SLADEK

A SEXUAL CONGRESS

Ödön von Horváth

PLAYS ONE

SLADEK

A SEXUAL CONGRESS

translated by

Penny Black

OBERON BOOKS
LONDON

First published in 2000 by Oberon Books Ltd.
(incorporating Absolute Classics)
521 Caledonian Road, London N7 9RH
Tel: 020 7607 3637 / Fax: 020 7607 3629
e-mail: oberon.books@btinternet.com

A catalogue record for this book is available from the British Library.

ISBN: 1 84002 133 0

Cover illustration: Andrzej Klimowski
Cover typography: Jeff Willis

Printed in Great Britain by Antony Rowe Ltd, Reading.

Contents

CHRONOLOGY

Titles have been given literal translations, unless there is a more famous alternative in English.

1901 9 December: Ödön (Edmund) Josef von Horváth born in Susak, a suburb of Fiume.
Father: Dr. Ödön Josef von Horváth, diplomat.
Mother: Maria Hermine, née Prehnal.

1902 Summer: family moves to Belgrade.

1903 6 July: brother Lajos von Horváth is born in Belgrade.

1908 Family moves to Budapest. First classes taught in Hungarian at home.

1909 Dr Horváth is called to Munich. Ödön stays in Budapest where he attends the *Rákóczianum* (archbishopal boarding school), and receives an intensive religious education.

1913 December: Ödön joins his parents in Munich.

1914 Ödön attends the *Wilhelmsgymnasium* in Munich. First differences with the religious education teacher Dr Heinzinger, which remain strong for years and later appear in Ödön's works. Dr Horváth is conscripted into the army.

1915 Dr Horváth is called away from the front back to Munich.

1916 Family moves to Pressburg. First attempts at writing, in the form of poetry, of which one, *Luci in Macbeth. Eine Zwerggeschichte* (A Dwarf Story) *von Ed. v. Horváth* survives. Friends of the time also tell of other 'occasional poems' eg *Professoren in der Unterwelt* (Teachers in Hades) etc.

1918 Before the end of the war Dr Horváth is called to Budapest. There Ödön meets a circle of young people (The Galileo Circle), who read the national-revolutionary works of Endre Ady with enthusiasm. Strong interest in the political power games in Budapest.

1919 Spring: Dr Horváth is called to Munich. Ödön is sent to his uncle in Vienna and attends the *Realgymnasium.* Summer: *Abitur* (A-Levels) in Vienna, then moves to Munich.
Autumn: Enrolled at the Ludwig-Maximillian University in Munich (until the winter semester of 1921/22).

1920 Meets Siegfried Kallenberg in Munich, who encourages him to write *Das Buch der Tänze* (The Book of Dances).

1922 *Das Buch der Tänze* published by *El Schahin* of Munich. Later, in 1926, Ödön buys all remaining books with the help of his father and destroys all available copies. 7 February: *Das Buch der Tänze* is shown together with *Buch der Frühen Weisen* (Book of Early Songs) and *Aus dem Herbst* (From Autumn) in the Steinicke-Saal in Munich, for the 'First Literary-Musical Evening of the Kallenberg-Society'. More attempts at writing, probably including *Ein Epilog* and the 'romantic novella' *Amazonas.*

1923 Ödön moves to his parents' country house in Murnau. Intensive period of writing, but he destroys most of his documents. Probably wrote the fragment *Dósa* and the play *Mord in der Mohrengasse* (Murder in Moor Street), incorporating ideas that were to appear in his later plays. As well as short prose texts he wrote *Sportsmärchen* (Sports Fairy Tales) which were published in various magazines and papers (1924 and later).

1924 26 March: on the occasion of the 'Third Literary-Musical Evening of the Kallenberg-Society' Ödön's plays are once again presented to the public, including *Geschichte einer kleinen Liebe* (The Trivial Love Story), *Ständchen* (Serenade)– with the music of Siegfried Kallenberg – and *Schlaf meine kleine Braut* (Sleep, My Little Bride) which has since been lost.
In autumn Ödön goes on a Paris trip for a several weeks with his brother Lajos, after which he decides to settle down in Berlin.

1926 20 February: *Das Buch der Tänze* has its premiere at the Stadttheater Osnabruck.
The popular play *Revolte auf Cote 3018* (Revolt on Gradient 3018) and the comedy *Zur schönen Aussicht* (The Belle Vue) were probably written around that time.

1927 In the office of the German League for Human Rights in Berlin, Ödön is sifting through papers for an account of the judicial crisis and finds material about the secret executions of the Black Army. Probably wrote the fragmentary play *Fall Ella Wald* (The Case of Ella Wald) around that time.
4 November: *Revolte auf Cote 3018* premieres in Hamburg. After the premiere, Ödön reworks his play and gives it the title *Die Bergbahn* (The Mountain Railway).

1928 Ödön visits Spain and uses his experiences there in the first part of his novel *Der ewige Spiesser* (The Eternal Philistine). He reworks his history *Sladek oder Die schwarze Armee* (Sladek, or The Black Army) and calls the new version *Sladek der schwarze Reichswehrmann* (Sladek, the Black Soldier).

1929 4 January: *Die Bergbahn* has its première in Berlin. The publishing company Ullstein offers him a contract which allows him to live as an independent writer.

Using an earlier work with the title *Ein Fräulein wird verkauft* (A Young Lady is Sold), Ödön writes the comedy *Rund um den Kongreß* (A Sexual Congress). The first chapter of the novel *Herr Reithofer wird selbstlos* (Mr Reithofer Becomes Unselfish) becomes the base of *Der ewige Spießer*. He also continues working on the stories of Agnes Pollinger, drawing from the concept of a '*Roman einer Kellnerin*' (Novel about a Waitress) with the titles *Ursula* and *Charlotte*. Probably starts on his novel *Der Mittelstand* (The Middle Class) around this time.
13 October: The matinée premiere of *Sladek* provokes strong attacks from the Nazis.

1930 Ödön finishes his novel *Der ewige Spießer* and hands it to the publishers Propyläen, whose drama department Arcadia also publishes his plays.
Several writer evenings, also in Munich.
People and events of his life reappear in his play *Italienische Nacht* (Italian Night).

1931 20 March: *Italenische Nacht* has its première in Berlin.
4 July: Oscar Sima directs a non-political version of the play in Vienna. At the premiere, Ödön explains that after a long period of work, he has just finished *Geschichten aus dem Wiener Wald* (Tales from the Vienna Woods).
22/23 July: Ödön is interviewed as a witness in a lawsuit and comes under strong attack from the Nazis.
Autumn: Following Carl Zuckmayer's recommendation, Ödön – together with Erik Reger – is given the Kleist prize.
2 November: The premiere of *Geschichten aus dem Wiener Wald* at the Deutsches Theatre in Berlin is an important success.
Max Reinhardt pushes Ödön and R.A. Stemmle to write a magazine *Magazin des Glücks* (Magazine of Happiness), together with Walter Mehring. Several drafts are made but never realised.

Ödön finishes his play *Kasimir und Karoline* the same year.

1932 February: meeting with Lucas Kristl in Munich, who inspires Ödön to write a play based on the personal columns in newspapers; *Glaube Liebe Hoffnung* (Faith, Hope and Charity) is based on a real story and reworked several times. Readings by the author in Munich and an interview in April with the *Bayrischen Rundfunk* (Bavarian Radio) are proof of Ödön's growing popularity.
18 November: Premiere of *Kasimir und Karoline* in Leipzig and a week later – the same production – in Berlin. Ödön begins to feel it necessary to write *Gebrauchsanweisung* (directions for use) for his plays.

1933 Heinz Hilpert is forced by the Nazis to put off Ödön's *Glaube Leibe Hoffnung* which he had agreed to premiere. The same happens for other productions of Ödön's plays in German theatres.
Ödön's parents' house in Murnau is searched by SA troops, causing the Hungarian ambassador to protest. Ödön leaves Germany, going to Salzburg and then Vienna.
Der Unbekannte aus der Seine (The Stranger from the Seine) is written.
In order to keep his Hungarian nationality, Ödön has to travel to Budapest. This inspires his comedy *Hin und her* (Back and Forth).
27 December: Ödön marries the singer Maria Elsner in Vienna. They are divorced the following year.

1934 The planned premiere in Vienna of *Die Unbekannte aus der Seine* does not take place.
Ödön returns to Berlin in order to study National Socialism as research for a new play. His impressions find their way into the draft and the scenes of *Der Lenz ist da!* (Spring Has Come!) The same concerns surface

later in his novel *Jugend ohne Gott* (Youth Without God). In Berlin, Ödön makes contacts in the film industry, develops various scripts, writes film dialogues and adapts subjects like *Kean* and *Brüderlein fein!* Records of this time have been largely lost but there are stories of works with titles such as *Kuss im Parlament* (A Kiss in Parliament) and *Pässe nach Deutschland* (Passports to Germany). Later Ödön distances himself from his work in film.
Using earlier material, Ödön writes the 'fairytale' *Himmelwärts* (Heavenbound), which is taken up by a Berlin company but cannot be produced in Germany. Ödön writes various drafts with different content using the same title, and also a novel (*Ludwig Schlamperl*). The Nazis start new investigations against him.
18 December: Premiere of *Hin und her* in Zurich. Ödön makes use of this opportunity to leave Germany together with the Berlin actress Wera Liessem.

1935 Several plans, drawings and fragments around the topic 'escape from the present' are written. Together with his brother Lajos, Ödön plans an illustrated epistolarian novel with the title *Die Reise ins Paradies* (Journey to Paradise) as a commission for publishers *Max Pfeffer*. Ödön writes the comedy *Mit dem Kopf durch die Wand* (With the Head Through the Wall) which he reworks several times until completely abandoning it after its premiere in Vienna (10 December).

1936 Ödön finishes the play *Der jüngste Tag* (Judgement Day) and rapidly, working from earlier drafts, he writes the plays *Figaro läßt sich scheiden* (Figaro Gets Divorced) and *Don Juan kommt aus dem Krieg* (Don Juan Comes Back from the War). During this time, Ödön mainly resides in Vienna and in Henndorf near Salzburg. When he visits his parents in Possenhofen in August, he is told that his residence visa has been withdrawn and that he has to leave Germany within 24 hours.

13 November: *Glaube Liebe Hoffnung* has its premiere under the title *Liebe, Pflicht und Hoffnung* in Vienna.

1937 Ödön distances himself from nearly all his earlier plays and decides to write a *Komödie des Menschen* (Comedy of Mankind). This leads him to write the comedies *Ein Dorf ohne Männer* (A Village Without Men) and the 'Komodie des Erdbebens' (Earthquake Comedy) *Pompeji*. These are the only two plays he is willing to include in his 'comedy of mankind'.
In Henndorf, Ödön writes the novel *Jugend ohne Gott*.
2 April: Premiere of *Figaro läßt sich scheiden* in Prague.
24 September: Premiere of *Ein Dorf ohne Männer* in Prague.
In autumn, *Jugend ohne Gott* is published by Allert de Lange in Amsterdam and becomes an enormous success; many foreign companies acquire the translation rights. Ödön starts his next novel *Ein Kind unserer Zeit* (A Child of our Times).
5 December: Premiere of *Himmelwärts* as a matinee show in Vienna.
11 December: Premiere of *Der jüngste Tag* in Mahrisch-Ostrau.
By the end of the year Ödön finishes *Ein Kind unserer Zeit* which is published by Allert de Lange.

1938 Severe depressions, dissatisfaction in his artistic life and financial worries stop Ödön from accomplishing further plans. He only writes a few pages of an idea for a novel called *Adieu Europa*.
March: His friends escape Germany: Walter Mehring to Zurich, Hertha Paula to Paris and Franz Theodor Csokor to Poland. Ödön leaves Vienna too, accepting Lajos von Hatvany's invitation to go to Ofen.
April-May: Having visited the actress Lydia Busch in Teplitz-Schönau, Ödön embarks on a series of journeys that eventually bring him to Paris on 28 May, where he has been invited for discussions with Armand

Pierhal, the translator of *Jugend ohne Gott* and *Ein Kind unserer Zeit*, and Robert Siodmak, who wants to make a film of *Jugend ohne Gott*.
1 June: Another meeting with Robert Siodmak. Ödön plans to travel to Zurich the next morning. Around 7.30 pm, he is killed by a falling tree, opposite the Marigny Theatre.
7 June: Ödön is buried in St Ouen cemetary, north Paris.

INTRODUCTION

Penny Black

At first glance *Sladek* and *A Sexual Congress* do not appear comparable bedfellows for a volume of Horváth plays. The former is a deeply committed political play showing how national events shape people, the latter a satirical and witty look at duplicity and double standards at an official level. However, a closer look at both plays reveals many similarities and not simply in their structure.

The first version of *Sladek* was written around 1927, a second, much shorter version was written as a stage script a couple of years later. This is a translation of the first play. In 1927 the German League of the Rights of Man issued a white paper on the failure of the judicial system in Germany. Horváth was involved in preparing the paper and so had access to the history of the illegal 'Reichswehr' and the so-called Feme murders. In particular, the case of Major Buckrucker, who planned in 1923 to march with his paramilitary group on Berlin and take over the government, seems to form the basis of *Sladek*.

A Sexual Congress was written in 1928 or 1929 and is probably based on two League of Nation congresses held in 1921 to examine prostitution and the white-slave trade. In 1927 a panel of experts appointed by the League of Nations advisory committee reported on the white-slave trade in twenty-eight countries, and according to the *Encyclopaedia Britannica* 'its report (1927) proved the existence of a highly organised and well-financed national and international traffic'. Horváth had been interested in the subject since his student days; whilst attending the University of Munich he had enrolled in a course on the campaign against prostitution.

So the underlying themes of both plays are deeply serious and concerned with greater humanity as opposed to individual stories. And this is reflected in the structure of the plays. Neither of them follows plot structure in the more traditional sense, but are rather a series of tableaux. In *Sladek* the action moves from outside in the square, via an apartment, an inn, a fortress and through the courtroom to the harbour. The placement of each scene allows for discussion and debate in that particular arena. A sense of menace stays with the protagonists from the moment the curtain rises on a political brawl almost to the very end, only absent from the final scene, which shows a pathetic Sladek spat out into a future more interested in entertainment than politics. At least there is a historical through-line, by *A Sexual Congress*, Horváth has taken the tableaux structure even further, scenes melt into one another, the place of each scene is less important, there are no dramatic turning points and the ending is contrived via *deus ex machina*, something Brecht was to use much later on.

In both of these plays the characters are subservient to the ideas they/ the author wishes to serve. In fact the protagonists on the political left in both plays assure us that 'an idea never dies'. And in *A Sexual Congress* the Marxist is shot and continues to survive and take part in the action as an idea. Nor do the characters relate intimately with each other: Sladek himself happily leads the guerrilla fighters to his lover, Anna, so they can murder her; in *A Sexual Congress* neither blood nor marriage ties mean anything to the dramatis personae.

So how does this work for an audience. Sitting in a darkened theatre watching protagonists we care not one jot about can be a depressing experience, yet the breadth and scale and scope of Horváth's vision draws us in. *Sladek*, with its aggression, its political skulduggery, its filmic-like demands on stagecraft, is pure political thriller with a profoundly moral end. The fact that Horváth is able to see a potential danger in the rise of the political right and Hitler already in 1927 says a lot for his vision and the blindness of others, and parallels can be drawn to present day Austria. On the other hand, *A Sexual Congress* dances through verbal arabesques, double-entendres and verbal minefields to highlight another serious issue yet in a wildly funny way. The 'International Congress for the International Fight against International Prostitution' is nothing more than a front and the play repeatedly shows us that in the battle between hypocrisy and honesty, hypocrisy always wins the day.

And this leads me to a brief mention of my approach to the translation of these plays. In listing the dramatis personae of *Sladek*, Horváth states that he wishes no character to be left out. This rather odd demand shows how keenly balanced Horváth felt the play was and that any exclusion or interference would throw it right off balance – and let us not forget, in his determination to get the play right he wrote two different versions of it. So in translating *Sladek* I have attempted to be as accurate as possible and have struggled to find the right phrase every time. I have not brought the play up to date linguistically – it was after all originally called a *Historie*. However in *A Sexual Congress* I have taken a much freer approach – jokes and puns do not do well when translated directly. Nor did I keep so closely to the historical context, as the signs are that hypocrisy today is still alive and kicking.

Penny Black
London, 2000

SLADEK

Characters

NURSE

FRANZ

KNORKE

SLADEK

ANNA

FRÄULEIN

SALM

HORST

RÜBEZAHL

HALEF

CAPTAIN

PARLIAMENTARY SECRETARY

JUDGE

PUBLIC PROSECUTOR

BARRISTER

LOTTE

PALM READER

POLICEMAN

NAZIS

SOLDIERS

SAILORS

GIRLS

ACT ONE

Scene 1

The end of a discussion

A street. NAZIS chase FRANZ out of a hall and beat him up; the music within is of the radical right 'Präsentier Marsch'.

It is night.

NAZI: Out. Kick the red dog out.
ANOTHER: Take that, and that, Jew boy.
NURSE: (*Appearing at the door.*) Who said that? Who said that we lost the war? Such comments have delivered the fatherland up to the disgusting lust of perverted sadists who then stab us, the victors, in the back. Syphilitic blacks are defiling German women on the banks of the Rhine. Oh yes, the German people have lost their honour. We must, we must win it back, even if another ten million German men die on the field of honour!
NAZI: *Heil!*
FRANZ: And you! Who are you to say the people have no honour? Who gave you the dubious right to demand ten million deaths? Madam, you are not human.
NURSE: Novemberling! Novemberling!
NAZI: Rip out his tongue. Rip out the tongue of the paid lackey!
KNORKE: (*Appearing at the door.*) Stop! Brothers of the alliance, do not besmirch yourselves with this filth. (*To FRANZ.*) Are you not the so-called editor, the pig, Franz, who…
FRANZ: (*Interrupting.*) Yes.
KNORKE: A pleasure to meet you in person. Now would you please be so kind as to answer the following trivial conundrum: your 'great' nation is breaking the Treaty of Versailles – your beloved 'peace treaty' – and is occupying the Rhine with flame-throwers. It is

proclaiming a republic on the Rhine, it wants to 'conquer' the whole nameless cheated German Reich all the way from the Maas to the Meml, from the Etsch to the Belt, despite the mighty protests of a wounded people.

FRANZ: The Treaty of Versailles is the work of imperialism, it is a declaration of war on the proletariat by international capitalists.

NAZI: Jews of all nations, unite!

KNORKE: You want the fatherland to become a French colony?

FRANZ: You know I don't.

(*The NURSE laughs.*)

I come from the occupied territories.

KNORKE: So do I.

FRANZ: French reactionaries are robbing the Ruhr of food and rights. A soldier is a soldier. The black, red and gold flag is alight.

KNORKE: Bravo!

NAZI: Bravo!

FRANZ: Bravo. And so the German proletariat reports for duty. But there are no weapons, there are no generals. The desire for peace is stronger than all the bayonets belonging to international reactionaries put together! Militarism will be smashed by the moral power of the worker, without bloodshed!

KNORKE: Headlines! Just ink!

FRANZ: Blood is blood!

KNORKE: And war is war! Passive resistance is the afterbirth of Jewish spite. A red cowardice! In Berlin international thugs lord it over the Jewish-Jesuit remains of the Weimar Republic. Brothers of the alliance. Soon the national army will march and mow down pacifist riff-raff in their path! Revenge for Strasbourg! Revenge for Schlesien! For Schleswig! For Schlageter!

NAZIS: *Heil! Heil!*

(*Song.*)

So my brothers join together
Raise your hands up high and swear
In our holiest alliance

For each other we'll be there.
The black on red of swastika
Will lead us through the night
Until our rifles are all empty
And we've won the freedom fight.
(*KNORKE, the NURSE and the NAZIS return to the hall, there are only four left.*)
Comrades, let us all shake hands
We'll stand firmly side by side
Even if we are defeated
Our fighting spirit will not hide.
A swastika is on our helmets
Band of black and white and red
We are Hitler's storm-troopers
That's what we are, alive or dead!

We will not allow, we will not allow
Old Ebert to rule over us!
Hey, Republic of Jews!
Hey, Republic of Jews!
Doctor Wirth will be hurt
Our guns fire tack-a-tack-a-tack
Onto the black and the red pack.
Kill old Walter Rathenau
The goddamned Jewish sow!
(*Suddenly there is silence.*
FRANZ leans against the wall and spits out blood.)

FIRST NAZI: He's had enough.

SECOND NAZI: Nowhere near enough, comrade.

THIRD NAZI: A circumcised Jewish pig is a decent man compared to an Aryan Jew-lover. It's just a nosebleed. A little warning.

SECOND NAZI: He'll bleed to death when hostilities resume.

FOURTH NAZI: And when will hostilities resume?

THIRD NAZI: Soon.

SECOND NAZI: When hostilities resume there'll be a law – every Jew has to buy himself a rucksack. Anything he can fit in it, he can take with him to Jerusalem. Anything he can't, belongs to us. Do you know how many Polish Jews are sprouting up all over Germany? Twenty million!

FIRST NAZI: There was only one Jew in our school. We didn't speak to him, but the bastard was clever. He was the only one in class who could translate Cicero and boy did we give him a hiding. He was black and blue all over and his glasses were smashed. His father, old Itzig, complained to the Rector, but he just said it was nothing more than the high jinks of youth and a good thing too – young boys who don't get into scraps don't make good soldiers. You see, we'd told the Rector that the Jewboy had been cheeky and that's why we thrashed him. He believed us. Are you dreaming?

SECOND NAZI: No. I was just thinking about the Jewish question. Yesterday I hit some barefoot Rebecca in the market because she'd said that the apples I sold her were rotten – filthy cow. People just laughed.

(*Calls of 'heil' and musical fanfares from the hall.*)

THIRD NAZI: The final speeches. Quick.

(*He runs back into the hall with the FIRST and SECOND NAZIS. The FOURTH NAZI walks slowly over to FRANZ. FRANZ hears him and turns around.*)

FOURTH NAZI: I didn't hit you.

FRANZ: Thank you.

FOURTH NAZI: Please. They nearly killed you in there and that would've upset me, because you are right and I love righteousness. You were quite right, we haven't lost our honour. But that's not what it's about. One just has to think for oneself. You are a so-called idealist.

FRANZ: And who are you.

FOURTH NAZI: My name is Sladek. You just have to think for yourself. I think a lot. I think all day long. Yesterday I was thinking, if I'd studied I could've been someone. I've a bent for politics. I'm a so-called retiring man. I only talk to people who think for themselves. I'm delighted to talk to you – you're also alone. I noticed that during the discussion. We're like brothers. I've thought about everything quite carefully, about the country, the war, peace, this whole injustice thing. You just have to realise there's only one quite specific rule. Always the same one. A quite specific rule, obviously, otherwise there'd be no point to anything. That is the great secret of the world.

FRANZ: Well?

SLADEK: Killings are plentiful in nature, that never changes. That's the meaning of life. That is the great rule. There is no reconciliation. Love is treacherous. Love is the great deceit. Me, I'm not afraid of the truth, I'm not a coward.

FRANZ: Neither am I.

SLADEK: I know. But there's a flaw in your reasoning. Don't laugh at me, please.

FRANZ: I'm not laughing.

SLADEK: You see, you ask yourself constantly how the human race can become happy. But that'll never happen, because, when all's said and done, there is only me. Me, Sladek. The human race doesn't love Sladek. And how things stand for Sladek is exactly how things are for the others. No one loves the masses. No one loves us – there's no such thing as love, anyway. We are hated. And alone.

FRANZ: What do you mean by we?

SLADEK: The fatherland.

FRANZ: And what do you mean by the fatherland?

SLADEK: When all's said and done – me. The fatherland is the country where you're born and where you stay, because you don't speak other languages. And all those theories of so-called Marxism don't concern me, because I can think for myself.

FRANZ: You think too much for yourself.

SLADEK: I have to. I have to. I mean, it is possible that the poor will rise up against the rich again, but I think all that's in the past. They slaughtered the reds. Many reds. You see, I was at Spartakus. Only in spirit, but I was there. It was then I heard the song about the heart beating to the left, but of course there is no heart, just a sort of muscle. Are you for this Republic?

FRANZ: There is no Republic as yet, it's to come.
SLADEK: It doesn't exist and will never exist, because it's built on a lie.
FRANZ: And on what lie might that be?
SLADEK: That reconciliation exists.
FRANZ: If reconciliation doesn't exist, then it has to be invented.
SLADEK: (*Smiling.*) You're not stupid.
FRANZ: Why? (*Pause.*) I never lie.
SLADEK: Killings are plentiful in nature, that never changes.
FRANZ: Nowadays the whole world is full of blood and filth.
SLADEK: I don't think about tomorrow. I just live for today. And today all nations are against us. They occupy our country, squeeze us dry. And as long as we have no weapons it won't change. There'd be no harm in a few million more dying, we're too many already. We're growing as if there'd never been a war. Soon the whole German Reich will be just one big city. We need our colonies back, Asia, Africa – there's too many of us. A pity the war's over!
FRANZ: You dare to regret the war is over?
SLADEK: Yes, I dare.
FRANZ: Are you human?
SLADEK: I am human, but there is always war.
FRANZ: There is also peace.
SLADEK: I can't remember peace.
FRANZ: I feel sorry for you.
SLADEK: Now you're lying.
FRANZ: Blinkered.
SLADEK: You see, I'm not afraid of the truth.
FRANZ: Were you a soldier?
SLADEK: No, I was twelve years old when war broke out. I just look older.
FRANZ: You should be muzzled.
SLADEK: It is quite possible that I will be muzzled one day. Because I know too much.
(*Silence.*)
FRANZ: Have you heard of the Black Army?
SLADEK: Don't mention that!

FRANZ: Aha! Why not?
(*SLADEK is silent.*)
I have heard that soldiers are gathering in the fields. They have cannons and machine guns and wear a cockade with the Eagle of the Republic upside down – shot down. Is that true?
(*SLADEK is silent.*)
I've also heard that these soldiers want to march victorious to Paris, trampling over the corpses of their own people.
SLADEK: That's none of your business!
FRANZ: That's where you're wrong! Very wrong. They call themselves the Black Army because they can only exist in secret. And anyone who betrays them is killed.
SLADEK: Killings are plentiful in nature, that never changes.
FRANZ: One should betray every army, soldier! (*He exits.*)
SLADEK: (*Alone – shouting after him.*) You're just a so-called conchie, traitor!
(*Song. From the hall.*)
Cheers, comrades, to horse, to horse
Through the fields to freedom ride!
Only there does a man have value
Only there is he filled with pride
With nobody there to help him
He stands there quite alone!

Scene 2

At Anna's

ANNA is sitting at her sewing machine. Outside on the street a wind-up organ is playing the national anthem. She stands up and closes the window. Someone knocks at the door. She goes to open it.

KNORKE: (*Entering.*) Good day. Could I speak to Herr Sladek?
ANNA: He'll be here any minute.
KNORKE: Are you Frau Schramm?
ANNA: Yes.
KNORKE: Pleased to meet you. Schramm-schrumm-schrimm-schrimm-schrumm-schramm. Wasn't that

a popular song about twenty years ago? Is your clock working? Is that the right time?

ANNA: Just about. Would you care to wait?

KNORKE: (*Sitting down.*) Five minutes to go. Sladek's usually punctual. Primadonna! Primadonna!

ANNA: He doesn't wear a watch.

KNORKE: And he can't sing either.

ANNA: Where did you meet Herr Sladek?

KNORKE: I can't remember.

ANNA: Have you known him for long?

KNORKE: Are you related to him?

ANNA: No.

KNORKE: Are you his landlady?

ANNA: Yes.

KNORKE: Nothing else? That's it?

ANNA: Why do you ask?

KNORKE: (*Reading the newspaper.*) The Mark's steady. Zurich is quoting twenty-two billion. Zurich lies on Lake Zurich. I was in China you know. (*He bangs the table, jumps up and runs about.*) Oh yes, in Eastern Asia, young woman! But nowhere have I met a people as good as the Germans. Retired bureaucrats should rebel! Just look at the papers! The Republic, mere henchman to foreign ambassadors, has the gall to demand that the last weapons be handed over! One signal from the entente and we are ready to castrate ourselves! I will personally stamp on the head of any bastard who dares to hand over one bullet until his conscientious soul flies up to his Jewish god! Please excuse my agitation – ah! Pictures of war! Who's that? He doesn't look happy about something.

ANNA: That's my husband. He didn't take a good photo, but then maybe that's how he felt at the time.

KNORKE: He fell?

ANNA: No.

KNORKE: I thought you were a widow?

ANNA: Missing. I'm no longer waiting, although occasionally a missing soldier does suddenly reappear. Russia is big, Siberia's a long way away.

KNORKE: Apropos Russia – have you read the new Polish newspaper?

ANNA: I don't read newspapers. Sladek's the one who reads them.

KNORKE: He reads a lot.

ANNA: Just the papers.

KNORKE: He knows a lot for his age. His views are a little muddled but on the whole, sound.

ANNA: Any spare time he has, he broods.

KNORKE: The new Polish newspaper is the height of calumny. They're all criminals.

ANNA: Who are?

KNORKE: The Poles. Every single Pole is a born liar!

ANNA: I don't think that individual Poles lie any more than individual Germans.

KNORKE: Oh no?

ANNA: It's about time the papers stopped agitating people against each other. There's no point.

KNORKE: You don't say!

ANNA: I think it's quite right that the Government wants all weapons to be handed in. It's a good law. We murdered each other for four years, and enough's enough. I'd point out every single hidden cartridge without hesitation.

KNORKE: I'd leave well alone if I were you.

ANNA: Why? Anyone who doesn't obey the Government should be punished.

KNORKE: Punishment requires force. And let me whisper this quietly in your ear – the Government doesn't have any. Anyway, what do you know about hidden ammunition?

ANNA: I know who you are and what you want.

KNORKE: Excuse me?

ANNA: I know you. I've seen you around.

KNORKE: Who am I?

ANNA: You come into town sometimes, in a car.

KNORKE: What sort of a car?

ANNA: I see everything.

KNORKE: What do you mean by everything?

ANNA: You want to turn Sladek into a soldier.
KNORKE: So?
ANNA: You're recruiting for the Black Army.
KNORKE: There is no Black Army.
ANNA: There is.
(*Silence.*)
KNORKE: I'm warning you.
ANNA: I beg you. I beg you, please – leave me my Sladek. It's so difficult to talk about. When a woman of my age hangs onto a man fifteen years younger than herself, it's always motherly and she doesn't want to let him out of her sight. Sladek is only a young man, he can't remember anything but war. He's so distrustful he can't even conceive peacetime. He has grown up in these 'great' times, I can see that. So I won't let him out of my sight, I have listened and I have spied – you can't deceive me. What is mine will remain mine.
KNORKE: Is Sladek your property?
ANNA: Yes.
KNORKE: No.
ANNA: Anyone I love belongs to me.
KNORKE: Does he want to belong to you?
ANNA: What do you mean?
KNORKE: Sladek has grown up and has changed his mind.
ANNA: Did he tell you that?
KNORKE: Ask him yourself.
(*Silence.*)
ANNA: Will you help me?
KNORKE: I'm warning you.
ANNA: I beg you, please don't tell Sladek that I know he wants to leave. Please, couldn't you tell him he is unfit to be a soldier? Tell him, please, please leave him for me. Your soldiers will march anyway, with or without Sladek, but me, I've already sacrificed everything for the fatherland. I can't bear to lose anything more. I'd betray the whole army to the Poles, today, if I had to.
KNORKE: I don't think so.
(*SLADEK enters, nods at KNORKE.*)

ANNA: The gentleman has been waiting some time. Where have you been?
SLADEK: I was angry.
ANNA: Who made you angry?
SLADEK: Are you happy now?
ANNA: Me?
SLADEK: Leave us alone, please.
KNORKE: Not necessary, Sladek. Frau Schramm has just asked me to inform you that you are unfit to be a soldier; if I don't, she'll betray everyone to the Poles.
SLADEK: Anna!
ANNA: Oh, that is so base.
KNORKE: I know you've kept your mouth shut, but Frau Schramm has been spying on you. And so Frau Schramm has forced us to take a good look at her character. Do you understand? Sladek, are you willing?
SLADEK: Willing.
KNORKE: Good. We'll meet at the Dark Lady. Goodbye.
SLADEK: (*Staring at ANNA.*) Goodbye.
(*Silence.*)
ANNA: And what dark lady might that be?
SLADEK: The Dark Lady. A bar.
ANNA: Don't lie!
SLADEK: Jealousy will turn you stupid.
ANNA: I don't care! Sladek! I'm so afraid for you. I see how greedily women look at you…
SLADEK: (*Interrupting.*) I'm faithful to you.
ANNA: No, you're only being considerate, in reality, you don't want me around any more. One day you'll simply go away and I'll look everywhere for you but find you nowhere.
SLADEK: Anna. Do you know what it means to betray an army to the enemy? Do you know what soldiers do to traitors?
ANNA: I don't care if they kill me.
SLADEK: They will kill you.
ANNA: It's up to you. Please stay, then I'll say nothing. Nothing. Do you know what it would mean to me if I lost

you? Stay, please, please. I beg you. I want you so much that I no longer have any shame. What are you thinking about now?

SLADEK: What I think bores you, you once said.

ANNA: No!

SLADEK: What I think is stupid, you said! That's what you said. I've a good memory, an excellent memory in fact.

ANNA: You remember everything.

SLADEK: Everything.

ANNA: And you forget nothing!

SLADEK: Nothing! Stop staring.

ANNA: I'm not staring. I only said you shouldn't think so much, because I don't understand politics. I can't keep up with you.

SLADEK: You just have to think for yourself. I came to you in rags. In my house they'd have killed you for one piece of bread. To me you were from another world, you had a two-room flat and drew a pension. You were a seamstress to the wives of salesmen. I could wash here. You bought me a winter coat. Thank you.

ANNA: It was my pleasure.

SLADEK: You are my first love.

ANNA: Don't be spiteful.

SLADEK: I'm not being spiteful. I just wanted to say that the first love plays a huge role in life. That's what I've heard.

ANNA: Sladek. You are already dead.

SLADEK: Why?

ANNA: (*Holding onto him.*) Say it. Go on, say it's all over. Over, over…

SLADEK: You say it.

ANNA: I can't. I'm so stupid. So stupid.

SLADEK: It isn't over.

ANNA: Oh, stop worrying about me! Don't torment me! Say it, go on, say it, let me go!

SLADEK: Fine. It is over.

ANNA: Look at me.

(*Silence.*)

SLADEK: There is no other way.
ANNA: There is.
SLADEK: You always know better.
ANNA: You cannot love, you can only be loving.
SLADEK: Isn't that enough?
(*Silence.*)
ANNA: (*Smiling.*) Don't look at me like that, my giant. My little giant. Stay, you'll stay. My young thing – it's so dark, the earth is still cold but the sun was warm once. The moon is rising.
SLADEK: This year there'll be no spring. There's nothing but clouds, clouds and clouds hanging over the ocean, mountains of them. They're all coming this way, that's what the newspapers say.
ANNA: It's not like that, it's different. Come on, give me a kiss... That wasn't a proper kiss. Like this, like this. (*She kisses him, then suddenly pulls away and steps back.*) What has got into you? What are you thinking of when I kiss you?
SLADEK: I don't enjoy such sensual kisses.
ANNA: You pig. You pig.
SLADEK: You're right, I am a pig. (*He exits.*)

Scene 3

In the wine tavern Zur Alten Liebe

SALM, HORST, HALEF, KNORKE and RÜBEZAHL are the only guests. The FRÄULEIN is serving them.

FRÄULEIN: The gentlemen are soldiers?
SALM: We just look like soldiers.
FRÄULEIN: I love a nice uniform. I'm from Metz. We had a lot of soldiers there. What a fine thing if there was another war!
HORST: It won't be long in coming, girl.
FRÄULEIN: Although I'd be quite happy if we just had some manoeuvres. So. You gentlemen are soldiers.
RÜBEZAHL: We are not soldiers, you stupid cow!

FRÄULEIN: Well, pardon me! Don't get so worked up, you daddy-long-legs. You are wearing uniform after all.

KNORKE: We just haven't taken them off since the war, that's all.

FRÄULEIN: Phooeee. That's disgusting.

HALEF: My dear girl, I might be no soldier but I am interested in manoeuvres and in certain particular exercises… (*He flirts with her.*)

KNORKE: (*To SALM.*) Her name's Schramm, Anna her rather dubious first name. She lives in the Prinzenstrasse number six and has attached herself to Sladek. She's of a dangerous age and probably prepared to die for her little boy.

SALM: Lovely night, tonight.

KNORKE: She knows everything, perhaps even what's in store for her. Yet she's prepared to hand every cartridge hidden in the Republic over to the Poles. Some woman.

SALM: Lovely night, tonight.

KNORKE: I understand, Lieutenant dearest, we understand each other like an old married couple. It is a very lovely night, tonight, and for some it will be the last.

SALM: What if Sladek doesn't come?

KNORKE: He'll come. He hates her.

SALM: Why?

KNORKE: Why does one person hate another? Either because he's given nothing or because he's given too much. She probably kept him. She must have been pretty horny at one time.

HORST: The whore should be beaten to death.

SALM: Could you beat her to death?

HORST: Of course – in the interest of the fatherland. We had a pure bred Doberman at home. One day I bound its legs together and beat it until my arm hurt. The dog didn't make a sound. That damned cur was so proud. Just looked at me.

SALM: You are so wonderfully unscrupulous, so divinely natural. It must be the vodka! My youth was wasted.

HORST: Please don't go all sentimental.

SALM: Of course not, I'm just sad thinking back. When you were six years old I was a housemaster in Siebenbürgen. The energy I wasted on the Romanian women there. I know, women hate men, there's plenty of examples in the animal kingdom. It wasn't until prison that I discovered my better self. I'm grateful to the war, it showed me a better way, and you, Horst, followed me.

HORST: Excuse me. Ideals made me leave my parents, not some sort of personal sentiment. I would've run away even without you – and to think I'd be doing exams now! What for? Actions count louder than understanding, weapons louder than words.

SALM: Don't be cruel.

HORST: Does the truth hurt? Do you put yourself above the fatherland? How you do deceive yourself.

SALM: And how the naughty boy torments me…

RÜBEZAHL: Salm. You have a face like Bruno Kastner, and I have no money. Hand it over.

SALM: Don't get drunk.

RÜBEZAHL: Pout at your young man and kiss my arse. Don't worry, my mouth's shut even when I am drunk. But I repeat, it would've been better if we'd killed the pig over at the fort and not beforehand in the woods – now we've got claret all over the car.

SALM: Be quiet.

RÜBEZAHL: There's only us, grandpa. We're the only guests. Well, have you got any money? What a dead place.

FRÄULEIN: The gentlemen came by car?

HALEF: We are travelling salesmen. We represent a large life insurance company. Our boss is a very distinguished Jewish businessman and that nineteen-year-old lad is his son.

HORST: I'm only seventeen.

HALEF: And just look at those hips.

SALM: Halef, there are some things that are just not funny.

HALEF: As you say, Majesty. I'm simply concerned that he is losing his modern figure.

FRÄULEIN: That shape is modern because of malnourishment and for no other reason. Because of the war.

RÜBEZAHL: Too true. There's barely a bosom to be seen.
FRÄULEIN: Are you blind?
HALEF: Yes, he is blind. I, on the other hand, can see only too well.
KNORKE: Me too.
HALEF: (*Embracing her.*) Hey look, as if there'd never been a war. I love peacetime. Do you want to come for a ride with me?
FRÄULEIN: No, that's far too dangerous.
RÜBEZAHL: (*Sharply.*) What do you mean?
FRÄULEIN: (*Waggling a finger at him.*) No you don't, you naughty man! You can't persuade me. I don't go for rides in the middle of the night with strange men – a matter of principle. I knew a chauffeur once, an Austrian, who invited me to a midnight party and then tried to rape me on a country road. I said, Sir, you have to desist and he said, you're nothing but a whore. And then he started swearing at me.
(*SLADEK enters.*)
Evening, sir.
SLADEK: (*Standing still.*) Evening.
KNORKE: Sladek! Over here! Well?
SLADEK: I'm here. I kept my word. I'm ready.
KNORKE: We're delighted.
SALM: Is there any petrol left?
HALEF: Three and a half drops. Not quite enough.
SALM: Go and buy the better stuff. Take Halef with you.
(*HORST and HALEF exit.*)
RÜBEZAHL: We'll need a new car soon.
KNORKE: (*To SLADEK.*) And how is your dear lady?
SLADEK: It's over. Well and truly.
KNORKE: Congratulations
SLADEK: Thank you.
(*The FRÄULEIN plays a gramophone – 'The Träumerei' by Schubert.*)
KNORKE: You know what happens to a woman who betrays soldiers to the enemy.
SLADEK: She hasn't betrayed anyone.
KNORKE: But she will betray us.

SLADEK: If she does betray us, then she deserves what's coming.

KNORKE: Should we wait until the enemy destroys us?

SLADEK: No, killings are plentiful in nature, that never changes.

SALM: We are nature.

KNORKE: And you too are part of nature.

SLADEK: Yes.

KNORKE: So?

SLADEK: So.

SALM: Let's get on with it.

KNORKE: You wait here. We just have to report in and we'll be back in two hours. Then we'll pay a visit to the lovely lady. Do you still have a key?

SLADEK: Yes.

KNORKE: Leave the downstairs door open. Understand? We'll wait downstairs for ten minutes, you'll hear a whistle and then we'll come up. We need that ten minutes, you'll have to make something up so she doesn't realise what's going on and then screams for help. She's very clever, but you know that. Tell her you've come back, you're sorry – you want to turn back the clock because you still love her, got that?

SLADEK: Yes.

SALM: Sladek, should you change your mind…

SLADEK: (*Interrupting him.*) You don't have to threaten me. I'm not afraid. I've thought it all through and I can think for myself. Everyone knows that.

SALM: Makes no difference.

SLADEK: Oho!

SALM: The bill! Time to go.

FRÄULEIN: All together?

SALM: We are one family.

RÜBEZAHL: His father is my son.

KNORKE: (*To SLADEK.*) See you in two hours then. (*He exits.*)

SLADEK: Bye.

SALM: (*To RÜBEZAHL.*) Up you get. Let's go or the captain will be upset. (*He exits.*)

RÜBEZAHL: (*Drinking up.*) Captain, sir! We need a new car. Maybe even a bus. (*He exits.*)

FRÄULEIN: Goodbye gentlemen. Goodbye. (*She starts adjusting her stockings.*)

SLADEK: (*Watching her.*) Goodbye.

FRÄULEIN: Do you know the gentlemen? They were soldiers, weren't they? No? Maybe? Say something. Are you dumb?

SLADEK: Yes.

FRÄULEIN: Men nowadays are so witty. What would you like? Shall we share a bottle of wine?

SLADEK: How much?

FRÄULEIN: A billion.

SLADEK: And how much do you cost?

FRÄULEIN: What do you mean?

SLADEK: Just tell me if I've got it wrong, but I heard you would undress for a billion.

FRÄULEIN: Some men prefer to drink wine.

SLADEK: I don't. I can't get drunk. I just bring it all back up.

FRÄULEIN: That bad, huh? Then maybe I'd better undress.

SLADEK: A billion is a lot of money.

FRÄULEIN: You a salesman?

SLADEK: I'm not a racketeer.

FRÄULEIN: You earn an honest wage?

SLADEK: No.

FRÄULEIN: A present?

SLADEK: No.

FRÄULEIN: It's really none of my business.

SLADEK: I stole the money. I know a widow who's got another three billion at home. She earns a decent wage and loves me. I mean, love doesn't exist. There's no such thing as love. You just have to think for yourself. It's a simple trade. She bought Sladek. I gave myself to her – but she's so jealous I don't get round to working. She wants to dominate me, that's why she let's me beg for every million. So now I've stolen a billion, it belongs to me and I'm in the right. Give me a cigarette.

FRÄULEIN: I like you more and more. Give me the billion.

SLADEK: Get undressed.

FRÄULEIN: Afterwards.

SLADEK: No, afterwards means I can be fleeced.

FRÄULEIN: I can see you've had dealings with some bad women.

SLADEK: Only with whores really.

FRÄULEIN: Ugh! Don't say that!

SLADEK: She knows I want to leave, but she doesn't know why. I'm too considerate to tell her. Everything must end. Well and truly, this time. Do you know what the worst thing is? When you want to but can't.

(*The FRÄULEIN laughs.*)

Don't laugh.

FRÄULEIN: But that's funny.

SLADEK: No it's tragic. Something died long ago, perhaps it never even lived, yet it's still being discussed as if it's alive and well. I'm not a coward, I never wanted to pretend, and yet I did. She knew that all she had to do was whimper and I couldn't resist. Because when all's said and done, I'm a decent man. But to take advantage of it is a crime.

FRÄULEIN: You can't be working much to have thought all that up.

SLADEK: I've never had a proper job. She didn't like to see me earn a living. She was afraid I could live without her. She preferred to look after me – the famous mothering instinct. Should be made a crime.

FRÄULEIN: (*Bending over him.*) Stop talking. It's going right over my head. Give me the billion.

SLADEK: Such beautiful skin…

FRÄULEIN: I'm a Sunday child.

SLADEK: I'm not. You're so soft.

FRÄULEIN: So is every woman.

SLADEK: No, not every.

FRÄULEIN: The little man has such big eyes. Look at me. Why won't you look at me?

SLADEK: I am.

FRÄULEIN: No, you're not.
SLADEK: I am.
FRÄULEIN: You're looking at me and yet you're not looking at me. I don't think you relate properly to women.
SLADEK: Very likely.
FRÄULEIN: Give me the billion, then I'll undress.
(*SLADEK gives it to her. She kisses him.*)
Thank you. (*She starts to undress for him.*) Thank you. You're a lonely man, you should come more often or you'll get melancholy. A woman is the pinnacle of creation.
SLADEK: Take all your clothes off.
FRÄULEIN: No, I'll catch a chill.
SLADEK: I gave you the billion and you promised…
FRÄULEIN: I promised nothing. Do you want me to catch my death?
SLADEK: What do I care? I won't be cheated.
FRÄULEIN: Don't you shout at me!
SLADEK: Down, oh pinnacle of creation.
FRÄULEIN: I'm not a dog, I'm a person. You! Out! Get out or I'll scream. I'll scream. This is no place for hatred. This is a place for love. (*She screams.*)

Scene 4

Anna's Place

She is lying in bed. A car stops on the street outside. She listens and sits up. SLADEK enters.

Pause.

ANNA: Evening, Sladek.
SLADEK: Evening, Anna.
(*Pause.*)
ANNA: I thought you were a soldier. And already in uniform.
SLADEK: No. Your nightdress. It's open, at the front.
(*ANNA quickly does it up.*)
Leave it.

ANNA: Yes, what does it matter.
SLADEK: Anna...I'm here because I want to come back to you.
ANNA: (*Staring at him.*) That's not true.
SLADEK: It is.
ANNA: (*Staring at him nervously.*) Where have you been?
SLADEK: With the soldiers. I've thought it all through.
ANNA: (*Standing up suddenly, she quickly throws a shawl around her shoulders whilst looking him square in the eye. She walks up to him.*) What do you want from me? What's in your mind now?
SLADEK: Everything's going to be fine.
ANNA: Impossible.
SLADEK: I love you.
ANNA: No. No.
SLADEK: I'm not lying.
ANNA: Earlier this evening you nearly killed me.
SLADEK: I never hated you.
ANNA: You have, and rightly so, quite rightly so. (*Pause.*) It's my fault. It wasn't right of me to hold onto you and not let you go, I thought I'd spend my whole life with you. I should have taken a step back long ago, but I was thinking only of myself. I tormented you. I was always in your way. I tried to control you, now it seems to me as if I had it all planned. Forgive me. Everything's clear now. Clear. As a bell. (*Pause.*) Go, please. There is no point in you staying here. You just imagine you feel something for me. It's over. Why am I not twenty years younger? Why did I have to meet you? It was pure chance. Life is cruel. No, not you – I took you, chained myself to you. I gave you everything, demanded everything. I was always looking for something – you didn't notice. You belong to another world. You see things differently, hear differently, think differently. Go, Sladek, go wherever you want. It's really not that beautiful here. I'm not stopping you. March off with your soldiers, I'm not going to hand over one single cartridge, and I am not going to the Poles. I won't betray anyone. Go, please go. I'll stay.
(*The whistle goes. SLADEK freezes.*)

You are young and I am old and grey. There's a whole century between us.
(*SALM, HORST, RÜBEZAHL appear and jump on ANNA.*)
SALM: Got you!
ANNA: Sladek! What is this! What is this!
RÜBEZAHL: This is this!
ANNA: Help! Help! Ow!
RÜBEZAHL: Aaah! How she wails!
ANNA: Sladek! Sladek!
SLADEK: Stop!
SALM: (*Pulling out his revolver. To SLADEK.*) Back off! Back off!
RÜBEZAHL: (*Throttling ANNA.*) Betray us! Betray us would you! Old cow!
ANNA: (*Collapsing whimpering.*) Ow, Sladek. You terrible man. You...you...you... (*She dies.*)
(*Silence.*)
SALM: (*To SLADEK.*) Put your hands up! What did you mean – stop!?
SLADEK: She was innocent.
SALM: Not possible.
SLADEK: It was possible.
SALM: Since when?
SLADEK: Since a couple of minutes ago.
SALM: Well?
SLADEK: It's not your fault.
SALM: And that'll save your skin, you idiot. Do you think...
SLADEK: (*Interrupting him.*) I'm not afraid. I'm not a coward. Killings are plentiful in nature, that never changes.
(*Voices from below.*)
HORST: I can hear someone.
SALM: Out now! Quickly!
RÜBEZAHL: What a filthy mess.
SLADEK: Well and truly.

End of Act One.

ACT TWO

Scene 5

The main HQ of the Black Army

A fort. SLADEK still in civvies. He enters the bunker with HALEF, HORST and RÜBEZAHL.

SLADEK: When do I get my uniform?
RÜBEZAHL: You'd look better in a dunce's uniform, traitor.
HALEF: With hanging straps and a row of medals. We are with mother nature. Three feet under the earth.
SLADEK: Isn't that six feet under?
HALEF: Maybe. Maybe that too. As I said.
RÜBEZAHL: I need a shave.
SLADEK: Is this the fort, the HQ?
HALEF: Yes, sir. And we are unborn souls. Waiting for the stork and hoping we won't be aborted. I talk a lot. Are you nervous too?
SLADEK: No.
HORST: It's been tipping it down, stopped now.
HALEF: Is it still raining? The one thing I wanted to be was a comedian. Get them laughing and put money in your pocket at the same time.
SLADEK: (*Seriously.*) That's very funny.
HALEF: Yes.
RÜBEZAHL: I'd like to go to a masquerade again. In tails and a starched shirt. Every so often I get stupid and want to be a great travelling salesman.
HALEF: Do you know what I dislike about the Fräulein? Her teeth are brown.
SLADEK: She has no soul. She's a cheat.
HALEF: Do you have a soul?
SLADEK: What is a soul?
HALEF: But you just said the Fräulein didn't have one.
SLADEK: Me?
RÜBEZAHL: You! In the name of the holy father's mother.

SLADEK: That's not what I meant.

HORST: Women are just bodies there to excite us.

SLADEK: If only they excited us and nothing else. For example, Anna...

RÜBEZAHL: (*Interrupting him.*) Keep your mouth shut! Just keep it shut!

HALEF: Sir. It is customary here not to talk about these things, at least not unofficially. You still have to learn the rules here.
(*Silence.*)

HORST: Is it still raining?

RÜBEZAHL: When all's said and done, it's the fault of the filthy Jews.

HALEF: Is it?

HORST: Yes.

SLADEK: When will I get my uniform?

HALEF: There are certain formalities to be dealt with first.

SLADEK: What sort of formalities? (*He stands up.*)

RÜBEZAHL: Stop! Where are you going?

SLADEK: I need to go.

HALEF: Stay there.

SLADEK: But I need to...

HALEF: Control yourself.

SLADEK: Why?

HALEF: We have orders to watch over one Sladek most carefully. You're our prisoner.

SLADEK: Prisoner?

HALEF: For the present.

SLADEK: And what crime have I committed?

HALEF: A very stupid one, idiot. What was it you said, you piece of meat? She was innocent, you said. And Salm has informed our Captain. There are many innocent people, you stupid bastard. Innocent people die of a throat infection, but that sort of thinking is dangerous, you stubborn mule.

SLADEK: Killings are plentiful in nature, that never changes.

RÜBEZAHL: How many times do you say that an hour?

HALEF: We are only talking formalities, but here such formalities are handled with care.

(*Silence. SLADEK has sat down again.*)

SLADEK: (*To HALEF.*) Are you Turkish?

HALEF: Me?

SLADEK: Yes, your name is Halef. I knew a Halef who sold Turkish honey. But then his name wasn't really Halef.

HALEF: I sell Turkish honey and was born in Saxony.

SLADEK: I've heard that Dresden is beautiful.

HORST: Who's been to Nuremberg?

RÜBEZAHL: Nuremberg is beautiful.

HORST: Yes. In the castle there's an amazing torture chamber. I visited it after my first communion with my grandmother, who lives in Nuremberg. She knows every single thumbscrew, she explained them all to me. My mother had stomach-ache, but me and my grandmother could only laugh. The Iron Maiden for example, is…

(*The CAPTAIN, SALM, KNORKE enter. RÜBEZAHL exits. He walks past the CAPTAIN without greeting him.*)

CAPTAIN: (*Stopping for a moment, he watches him leave, then quickly walking up to SLADEK, who has stood up.*) Sladek, I have heard that you believe that the traitor Anna Schramm was executed when she was, in fact, innocent.

SLADEK: She didn't want to betray anyone, she told me so, I don't generally believe women, but this was out of the ordinary.

CAPTAIN: So, you're saying she was innocent?

SLADEK: Yes.

CAPTAIN: So.

SLADEK: There is no so. Nothing can be done about it now.

CAPTAIN: But what if something could be done.

SLADEK: That's not possible.

CAPTAIN: You shouted 'stop'. Are you aware that in some circumstances 'stop' could halt the entire revolution?

SLADEK: I wasn't thinking of the revolution, I was thinking about righteousness. It was as if I'd suddenly realised that my views on nature were wrong, and that I'd forgotten the truth. I can think for myself.

CAPTAIN: Shut up! You are not to think for yourself. You are a soldier. It takes three thousand Sladeks to make up a regiment. You're just one component. Components that think for themselves are surplus to requirement, thus dangerous and so will be destroyed. Is that understood?

SLADEK: Yes.

CAPTAIN: And with regards the innocence of your Anna Schramm: for the sake of the fatherland, every soldier bears the guilt for every crime. Every time.

SLADEK: I just couldn't help it.

CAPTAIN: You have to help it. That is your duty. Do you know what your duty is? Obedience. Without question. Should you ever consider shouting stop again, I will lock you up until Christ's Second Coming. And you know where. Dismiss! (*He leaves him standing there.*)

SLADEK: (*To HALEF.*) May I leave now?

HALEF: You may. Halt! Do you believe in the Second Coming?

SLADEK: No, I'm not a religious man. (*He exits.*)

CAPTAIN: (*To SALM.*) You brought that cripple with you, now look after him.

SALM: Thank you.

CAPTAIN: He's already shown himself to be out of the ordinary – and he can think for himself!

SALM: I know he's stupid, but better an idiot than a coward. I knew his brother, we were neighbours in Tsingtau before the war. He was very clever and well-schooled, but he was hanged on the battlefield for shooting his sergeant in the back during a charge. The Sladeks are all very bitter. They've come down in the world.

CAPTAIN: And I just have to say it again. That last execution was handled with such stupidity I can hardly believe it. Were you all drunk?

SALM: We'd not had a drop.

CAPTAIN: Then you were generous to a fault. I am surrounded by traitors, but I only ever catch the vanguard – I never get to the command.

(*The PARLIAMENTARY SECRETARY appears. SALM, KNORKE, HALEF, HORST leave. Silence. The CAPTAIN glares at the SECRETARY for a while.*)

CAPTAIN: You've come from Berlin?

SECRETARY: From the competent authority.

CAPTAIN: As you can see – I am ready.

SECRETARY: Thank you.

CAPTAIN: But is the competent authority still sleeping? They might well wake up under a Soviet sky.

SECRETARY: Political responsibility means waiting for the most suitable moment to attack.

CAPTAIN: I'm waiting.

SECRETARY: We already have a list of ministers but there are unresolved issues with the leaders of certain committees.

CAPTAIN: I'm waiting.

SECRETARY: North and South are still not in agreement!

CAPTAIN: I'm waiting. For the time being, anyway.

SECRETARY: We know, that's why I'm here.

CAPTAIN: Delighted!

SECRETARY: You are a man whose own position occasionally has to be made clear to him. You and your solders are under the command of the competent authority, which has been forced to…

CAPTAIN: Thank you. The competent authority is cowardly. It is praying for a national revolution yet recoils from any firm decision. I put it down to the air in Berlin.

SECRETARY: And the Prussian government.

CAPTAIN: It will happen, as it did in Hungary.

SECRETARY: The dictatorship. Plebs are still plebs. If there were no blacks on the Rhine and no inflation, then our dear fellow Germans would be like pigs in black and red shit.

CAPTAIN: Never. I believe in a second war of liberation. When the Republic collapses, so will the Treaty of Versailles.

SECRETARY: Hardly.

CAPTAIN: Oho!

SECRETARY: Hardly, Captain. Our troops and above all our weapons only suffice to beat back the domestic enemy, but not the external one. The national dictatorship will have to continue with the policies of Rathenau and Genossen. We might preach to the contrary but that's just propaganda. We're not actually lying, because when all's said and done, anything is possible.
(*Silence.*)

CAPTAIN: I see, once again someone is playing a dishonest game with me. I believe that in order to protect the Republic, the competent authority would even go so far as to hand me over to the Federal Court of Justice.

SECRETARY: If you started thinking about existing officially without permission, yes.

CAPTAIN: If it all went wrong, I wouldn't think twice. My national loyalty would be called upon and I'd take responsibility for everything. Even justice.

SECRETARY: What do you mean, even justice?

CAPTAIN: Don't play the untouched virgin with me, coward. People like you should dress to the political left. Please send my best wishes to the competent authority: and if your idiotic head teachers and ossified ministers of the unions and brotherhoods and committees and councils don't come to some agreement soon, then I will begin to exist! Without my help the national movement is nothing more than a debating society! I have gathered the troops! I have the force! I am the power! I will march even if I am alone! I am the national revolution, me and my comrades, the country boys have rescued the state once already, we killed Spartacus, we fought in the Baltic and in Oberschlesien. And now we will not allow ourselves to be…
(*The PARLIAMENTARY SECRETARY smiles sarcastically, bows stiffly and leaves at speed. The CAPTAIN is alone, he stares after him. He walks up and down. A trumpet sounds. He stops and listens. He grins.*)
I'll march. I'll march…

HALEF: (*Entering.*) Captain!

CAPTAIN: What!

HALEF: Salm wants to know what to do with the man who confiscated the post yesterday – he's lying downstairs. He's confessed to wanting to betray us to the allied board of control for fifty dollars.

CAPTAIN: He's lying. That man wouldn't betray anything for fifty dollars. I saw that straightaway. Something else drives him. We'll have to interrogate him with particular care.

HALEF: Shall we beat him up again?

CAPTAIN: Who beat him up?

HALEF: I didn't.

CAPTAIN: Who then?

HALEF: Rübezahl.

(*Silence.*)

CAPTAIN: Halef, is it true that Rübezahl threatened to shoot me down if I don't pay him?

HALEF: He was drunk.

CAPTAIN: Drunk or sober! Did you hear it with your own ears?

HALEF: I was there.

CAPTAIN: I have to insist that such matters are reported to me immediately.

HALEF: Quiet, Captain, quiet. Would you dare to punish such a commendable man, and if you dared, could you actually carry it out? No. You would only look ridiculous. Nothing more.

RÜBEZAHL: (*Appearing.*) Majesty, I've been listening at the door. (*He grins.*)

CAPTAIN: You'll get what's coming to you.

RÜBEZAHL: Sounds fun.

CAPTAIN: Dismiss!

RÜBEZAHL: Are you threatening me? You? Me!

CAPTAIN: No, I'm just a little concerned you might shoot me down.

RÜBEZAHL: (*Grinning.*) Don't be afraid, little dwarf.

CAPTAIN: Leave! Now!

RÜBEZAHL: Shut your barking, Doberman. Shut your barking or I'll wrap your belt so tight around your gob you'll be saying your prayers for real.

(*The CAPTAIN glares at him, controls himself then exits at speed.*)

Scene 6

Still underground in the bunker

FRANZ is leaning against the wall. The CAPTAIN comes in. SLADEK follows him with his bayonet at the ready and then stands on guard at the door.

CAPTAIN: So, you've confessed to passing on information on secret armaments to the French spy centre for fifty dollars.
FRANZ: Are you in charge here?
CAPTAIN: Yes.
FRANZ: Am I to be beaten again?
CAPTAIN: I will not apologise for the fact that you've been badly treated, but I do condemn it.
FRANZ: I demand to be dealt with by a proper court.
CAPTAIN: You will be punished in accordance with the proper laws.
FRANZ: I demand to be judged according to the penal code.
CAPTAIN: As long as the penal code is censured by the allied military command, then in the name of the German people, I am the proper court.
FRANZ: You have no right.
CAPTAIN: Don't be a fool.
FRANZ: Then kill me now. What do you want from me anyway?
CAPTAIN: You will not be killed.
FRANZ: Sorry, beaten to death.
CAPTAIN: No, you will be pardoned. With one proviso.
FRANZ: If I am pardoned, then it is without proviso.
CAPTAIN: I am in command here.
FRANZ: Don't be an idiot.
CAPTAIN: I am not in the habit of being an idiot. I forbid such impudence. I am in command here.
FRANZ: I would just like to point out that you can't let me go. I might betray all your secrets the moment I'm set free.
CAPTAIN: The moment you're set free there won't be any more secrets. I'm waiting for a signal from the competent

authority. Tomorrow or the next day. As soon as we march, you're free to go. My word of honour. With the one proviso.

FRANZ: Which is?

CAPTAIN: I know who you are. I too have my spies. It's not true that you'd betray the fatherland for fifty dollars. You'd have done it for nothing. You're an agent of the Third International.

FRANZ: No.

CAPTAIN: Don't lie. You're just pretending to be a traitor to protect your comrades. My proviso is this: lead me to the Communist's munitions dump and you're free to go.

FRANZ: The Communists don't have any weapons left. Spartacus is dead.

CAPTAIN: There is no Red Army?

FRANZ: In Russia, maybe.

CAPTAIN: What about Germany?

FRANZ: No. There is only a black one or a white one. I am not an agent of the Third International. I fight against every terror, even a red one.

CAPTAIN: What with?

FRANZ: With the power of ideas.

CAPTAIN: Fool.

FRANZ: Thank you.

CAPTAIN: You're a so-called conscientious objector.

FRANZ: Yes.

CAPTAIN: You betray as a matter of principle.

FRANZ: A matter of principle.

CAPTAIN: Your own army.

FRANZ: Any army.

CAPTAIN: No, only the German one. The criminals of Versailles.

FRANZ: I hate Versailles.

CAPTAIN: But you'd betray German soldiers to the signing up committee?

FRANZ: No. I don't know of any such committee. I don't know any German soldiers, I only know reactionary mercenaries whose secrets I wanted to divulge – they aim at Versailles but hit the German people. They and Versailles are responsible for the same thing…

CAPTAIN: You really are a fool!

FRANZ: You only have five thousand men. Do you really think that you can rip up the Treaty of Versailles with five thousand men and without heavy artillery, without planes, without tanks or any other murderous weapons?

CAPTAIN: If I did not have the Black Army, then the fatherland would have been occupied by the enemy long ago.

FRANZ: You're forgetting that you're a secret. How can the enemy be afraid of soldiers it doesn't even know exist? Sir! You are marching against your own people. Against the German Republic.

CAPTAIN: And what is the German Republic? The Republic is the whore of Jews and Jesuits. You are a so-called conscientious objector. That means, a bastard without any sense of responsibility for the fatherland.

FRANZ: I am a conscientious objector. That means: the strongest possible sense of responsibility for the individual.

CAPTAIN: (*Shouting.*) And betrayal of the fatherland! The individual is nothing!

FRANZ: (*Shouting.*) We are talking about millions of individuals. The people are the fatherland and war is the greatest crime against the people. What the people have rebuilt is being destroyed by the cold ambition of professional solders and by the thoughtless calculations of mad mercenaries. Your calculations are all wrong. Accounts have already been settled and the traitors sentenced. Soon judgement will be executed in the name of the Republic. It might not be much of a Republic yet, but it soon will be.

CAPTAIN: War is a law of nature.

FRANZ: And if it were a law of nature, I would fight nature itself. I am lining up the anarchy of destruction against the law of rebuilding, order versus chaos. You want to go back, I want to move forward. You want a national dictatorship, to sink back into the slime of base instinct –

you will fail, no matter how convinced you are that you are right. I set the global nation state against the criminal madness of robber nations. I fight using words as weapons. You can kill me, but it is a fact that ideas never die. Your weapons are already rusting and will soon turn to dust. Your time as a robber-knight has collapsed amidst blood and filth – your day has come and gone. It is now deepest night. He who survives the night will live to see the dictatorship of human rights.
(*Silence. The CAPTAIN stares at him fixedly.*)

CAPTAIN: You have over extended yourself. I let you carry on. Do you still dare to deny you are one of Moscow's agitators?

FRANZ: I have no connection whatsoever to Moscow.

CAPTAIN: So you don't want to abide by my proviso?

FRANZ: I don't know of any Communist arsenal.

CAPTAIN: Don't lie, you coward!
(*Silence.*)

FRANZ: Is it not cowardly to kill me?

CAPTAIN: We are talking of the fatherland.

FRANZ: You consider yourself to be the fatherland?

CAPTAIN: (*Almost slightly unsure.*) I fight for the fatherland. For its greatness, for its power. How can you understand? Germany can only be healed under a national dictatorship. Your view of the world is rubbish – perhaps a lovely dream. I don't worry about such things. I'm a soldier. I don't dream.
(*Silence.*)
I'm offering you one last chance. Do you agree to my proviso?

FRANZ: I can't. I'm not a communist. I don't belong to any party. I am alone.

CAPTAIN: You lie. Why did you say that you would betray us for fifty dollars if you weren't trying to protect anyone?

FRANZ: I lied because I knew that would be the end. If I had said I was a conscientious objector and no ordinary traitor then I would have been beaten for longer. I wanted to be killed as quickly as possible. It was pure egotism.

CAPTAIN: Pacifism is egotism.

FRANZ: (*Right.*) As you know, I am here purely for my own personal pleasure.
(*Silence.*)

CAPTAIN: You are mad. A danger to the public.
So, madman, do you believe there will ever be peace?

FRANZ: No, I don't. (*He wavers somewhat.*)

CAPTAIN: (*Agitated.*) Don't you make a fool of me.

FRANZ: I am not making a fool of you. I believe we understand each other. From your point of view you're absolutely in the right – but how high is your point of view, do you want to stand above or below it – and how close can you stay to it... (*He holds his head in his hands.*) I beg you, please stop the interrogation – for a short while. My head is so heavy. I was hit about the head which is what happens if... (*He smiles and sits down.*)

CAPTAIN: (*Staring at him. Then turns suddenly.*) Sladek!

SLADEK: Yes, sir!

CAPTAIN: Should the others return, my orders are that no one is to interrogate this man. Understood?

SLADEK: Yes, sir!

CAPTAIN: I am the only one doing the interrogating here. (*He exits.*)
(*Silence.*)

SLADEK: (*Suddenly.*) They won't hit you any more now.

FRANZ: (*Looking at him astonished, mockingly.*) I am deeply grateful.

SLADEK: I too am grateful, that you didn't give me away.
(*They look at each other. SLADEK smiles.*)
Yes, thank you for not letting on that you know me. It could have made things difficult. They might have become suspicious. Without reason. We might know each other but we think very differently.

FRANZ: How's that?

SLADEK: You know.

FRANZ: No.

SLADEK: I don't believe you.

FRANZ: Who are you?

SLADEK: Who am I?

FRANZ: Yes, you.

SLADEK: You don't remember me?
FRANZ: No.
(*Silence.*)
SLADEK: I recognised you straightaway. I'm Sladek.
FRANZ: Sladek? I don't know any Sladek.
SLADEK: We had a discussion once. When they almost beat you to death, which I wasn't very happy about because of my belief in righteousness – even though it doesn't exist. We had a debate, I really only like talking to intelligent people who can think for themselves – even though one shouldn't. In truth, I'm a so-called retiring man. I remember every word.
FRANZ: Aha, that discussion! But I don't remember you.
SLADEK: I'm sorry you've forgotten me.
FRANZ: (*Almost mockingly.*) I do apologise, but I know so many people…
SLADEK: (*Interrupting him.*) Please, please. The individual doesn't count, that's quite right, although it can lead to some odd experiences.
(*Silence.*)
FRANZ: What did we talk about?
SLADEK: That's not easy to say. We talked about killings in nature, that'll never change, about reconciliation, that'll never happen, and about justice, which doesn't exist – but, as I said, can lead to some odd experiences. We debated world politics. Your nose was bleeding.
(*Silence.*)
I'm glad you said you don't believe there'll ever be peace, there'll only ever be violence. That you converted to my way of thinking about the meaning of life.
I'm glad, because you are a so-called intelligent man.
Are you listening?
FRANZ: (*His head in his hands – apathetically.*) Yes.
SLADEK: I'm glad to talk to you again, I hardly have any opportunity to talk here because one is not allowed to think for oneself. Perhaps it's better so, but I can't help myself. Unfortunately, perhaps.
(*Silence.*)

An intelligent man admits it when he's wrong. I too think somewhat differently today. Although I was always right, it was all a bit confused. I made the mistake of thinking I was the centre of the world. Me, Sladek, whereas in fact Sladek is only one component. I mistook myself for the fatherland.
(*Silence.*)
I've thought everything through very carefully. The individual is only one part of the fatherland and this individual should not murder, for example. However people are always being murdered, because that's the way it is, but only the individual as component is allowed to murder, even though, when all's said and done, everything is for the individual. The funny thing is that if one becomes too independent as a component, for example when it comes to murder, one feels one should be doing the opposite, although one has no choice.
It's all very complicated. (*Pause.*) Are you listening?

FRANZ: (*As before.*) Yes.

SLADEK: Such is life. That's where you're wrong: you say you respect the individual parts. Whoever follows that through to the end has to kill himself, because killings are plentiful in nature. Just like in the Republic, if you do not kill you will be killed. Without murder there is not life, it cannot continue. And it has to continue.
It might not get any better, but you never know.
The individual parts don't count for anything by themselves, we must only think of the whole. (*Pause.*)
For example, the individual may as a part of the whole kill anyone if it is for the fatherland. Any time. I was there once when a traitor was killed for the fatherland.
A woman.
(*FRANZ pricks up his ears.*)
I'm only telling you this because you're an intelligent man and, as I said, I don't have much opportunity to discuss things here.

FRANZ: Go on.

SLADEK: A traitor to his country has to be dealt with in the interest of everyone else, that's quite clear. Everything was fine, even if she might have been innocent, we couldn't have done anything else, we had to execute her, that's just how things are sometimes. Even the innocent have to die for the whole, nothing changes. We were in the right. This is for your ears only because, as I said, you think for yourself and so maybe can understand. I understand everything, what I don't understand is why I sometimes feel that those who killed the woman, although in the right because they couldn't have done differently, did something wrong. It is very interesting.

FRANZ: Very. (*Pause.*) Who was this woman?

SLADEK: That's a secret. This whole thing is just between us…

FRANZ: You think so?

SLADEK: It was for your ears only, please.

FRANZ: Why?

SLADEK: Just between us two. Us two.

FRANZ: (*Mockingly.*) Thank you for your trust.

SLADEK: You won't give me away?

FRANZ: Why not?

SLADEK: Sorry?

(*Silence.*)

FRANZ: Walking up to him. You give yourself away. As a part you think too independently, that's why people like you go stupid. Now I know who you are.

SLADEK: Only now?

FRANZ: You are Sladek.

SLADEK: Yes.

FRANZ: That's very interesting. I also know who your 'traitor' was.

SLADEK: Who?

FRANZ: Her name was Anna.

SLADEK: No!

FRANZ: Yes! And her henchman's name was Sladek!

SLADEK: Don't lie!

FRANZ: It is all very interesting, Herr Sladek. The courts have no idea that this crime was an 'execution in the interest of the fatherland.' Police view it as a murder, a very independent murder.

SLADEK: I'm no murderer.

FRANZ: Killings are plentiful in nature, that never changes. The police say, as you, sir, can read in any newspaper, that it was a despicable subject called Sladek who abused the motherly love of an older woman in the most egoistic manner. A workshy skinflint, who let her look after him and who wasted her pitiful savings, which he stole from the cupboard, on whores. And when she couldn't bear it any more, he murdered her in a most bestial fashion. Other inhabitants of the house heard Frau Schramm shout 'Sladek!' and then they found her murdered. The state prosecutor has offered a reward for the capture of the murderer.

SLADEK: How much?

FRANZ: A lot.

(*Silence.*)

SLADEK: None of it is true. It was all quite different.

FRANZ: It was all for the fatherland?

SLADEK: Yes, but there is no justice.

FRANZ: Maybe there isn't. But as long as there are independent-minded Sladeks, there will continue to be police and judges.

SLADEK: It is terrible to be able to think.

CAPTAIN: (*Entering.*) I see you are already feeling better – Sladek! What did he want of you? Are you deaf, idiot?

SLADEK: He was just asking when he'd be interrogated again.

CAPTAIN: Now. You deceived me. You didn't need to recover from anything.

FRANZ: I did not deceive you.

CAPTAIN: What an actor. You wanted to break off the interrogation because you were contradicting yourself and had lost the plot. I'm not going to let it go. At issue is your statement – you don't believe there will ever be peace. And you are arrogant enough to try and convince me you are not an agent of Moscow and that you fight solely with the 'weapons of ideas', that you are a conscientious objector and preach eternal peace. What do you say?

FRANZ: The fact that this apparent contradiction is causing you to think hard is probably more due to your unfounded agitation at being deceived than to a well-founded feeling you've been apprehended.

CAPTAIN: I will not permit this!

FRANZ: You understand me, I've said that already. Because you are fully in agreement with me, but you cannot bear hearing what you are truly thinking and so you want to force me to maintain the opposite.

CAPTAIN: You really are mad!

FRANZ: Yes, and a danger to the public. And with regards eternal peace, I don't really believe in it but I preach it, because, when all's said and done, I do believe in progress. I know there can only be progress if the individual is not considered. When all's said and done, everything hinges on the individual, that's why I preach the most radical step, an empire of the faceless masses. There will be no progress as long as there are individuals. You are the dictatorship. You do not preach peace. You declare war and don't believe in progress. Neither do I. But perhaps there can be progress and you and I are deceiving ourselves. That's possible, no? You feel it's your duty to step down or fanatically maintain the opposite, otherwise you will go mad with doubt or pride. At a certain point we have to stop thinking, that's an unwritten law. It is not my duty to destroy an individual's desire for peace. It is my duty to deceive. And when all's finally said and done, I'd say that it is not deception, because nothing depends on mankind's actual state of affairs, but on how the individuals think they're feeling. Do we understand each other?

CAPTAIN: No, I am not a deceiver. The national dictatorship will win back the proud position of the German fatherland on the world's stage, despite all allied powers! That is my belief!

FRANZ: And is that not deception?

CAPTAIN: I will not permit this!

FRANZ: You are convinced that winning back the so-called proud position on the world's stage is, when all's said and done, an improvement?

CAPTAIN: I am not interested in the 'when all's said and done'.

FRANZ: You see!

CAPTAIN: What?

FRANZ: This 'when all's said and done' hinges upon you as an individual. That must be clear to you.

CAPTAIN: What do you mean?

FRANZ: I've already told you – the era of the robber-knight is over – your era. You will fail as you have to fail.

CAPTAIN: You don't say. Are you a prophet?

FRANZ: I believe I know that for sure.

CAPTAIN: Then you are deceiving yourself.

FRANZ: (*Smiling.*) Perhaps 'when all's said and done'. But 'when all's said and done' it's none of my business whether you belie your position or not.

CAPTAIN: What position?

FRANZ: Whether higher or lower. You have no right to act according to your perceptions without any consideration for others. Perhaps I am wrong – maybe you don't have any sense of duty at all.

CAPTAIN: What nonsense. You idiot. You philosopher. And as for my era, which you call the robber-knight era, the final proof lies in my fist!

FRANZ: (*Smiling.*) When all's said and done.

(*Silence. HALEF enters.*)

HALEF: Captain.

CAPTAIN: Out! Did you hear, get out!

HALEF: Don't be stupid, Captain. We are surrounded.

CAPTAIN: Surrounded! Who? Us!

HALEF: (*Walking right up to him, downcast.*) Us. Don't stare.

CAPTAIN: But who has surrounded us?

HALEF: The others. They crept up in the night. When daylight came our sentries spotted them. They've brought artillery with them. The whole fort is surrounded.

CAPTAIN: What sort of soldiers?

HALEF: Regulars.

CAPTAIN: Regulars?

HALEF: They've sent a delegation with a white flag, as though we were at war. Something stinks, Captain.

(*The CAPTAIN runs out.*)

Scene 7

Open Fields

The PARLIAMENTARY SECRETARY and two regular SOLDIERS with white flags are waiting for the CAPTAIN. The morning is grey. The CAPTAIN arrives with HALEF, stops without saying a word and glares at the PARLIAMENTARY SECRETARY.

SECRETARY: (*Bowing slightly.*) Captain. The competent authority has ordered me to inform you of their decision with regards your future deployment, if I can put it that way. Your army, if I can call it that, will be sent firstly to guard the border, as there is concern that irregular enemy troops might attack; secondly, as a kind of emergency police force with the task of collecting weapons hidden across the country; and thirdly, to fight alongside regular soldiers in case of a Bolshevik uprising. The domestic political situation has rather surprisingly been consolidated, so the existing means of power are more than sufficient to deal with a left-wing revolution, which is looking unlikely, on the other hand the foreign political situation…

CAPTAIN: Lies. All of it. This is a scandal. My soldiers are soldiers, not policemen and not nightwatchmen. They are the army of the national revolution. We came together not to protect this state but to crush the Republic underfoot. We will fight for a national dictatorship and not for some bastard international democracy!

SECRETARY: …On the other hand the foreign political situation offers, if not reconciliation, then at least the possibility of economic rapprochement of nations, so, in our own national interest and despite all humiliation, we Germans have to walk this path so that a solid economic base for our citizens can be established. The competent authority had therefore to make a decision – and they did not make this decision lightly – that your army, if I may call it that, is to be disbanded immediately. The competent authority will do everything in its power to find respectable civilian occupations for your people.

CAPTAIN: Thank you.

(*Pause.*)

I was expecting to be betrayed – again. We will manage without the respectable civilian jobs, one has to be born into that sort of thing. There is no way that I will obey the criminals who would betray the German ideal, even if they do view themselves as the competent authority! Tell them that I don't give a damn about economic rapprochement for our citizens, that I don't believe in reconciliation and that I will fight until Germany is feared once more!

SECRETARY: I must point out to you – if you don't disband voluntarily then we have the right to use force. In whatever circumstances using whatever means! The well-being of the German people is more important than your country boy ambitions. You are surrounded and…

CAPTAIN: With artillery! I will not give in. You crept up in the middle of the night and wanted to catch me unawares, I will break through in broad daylight and carry our flag to Berlin!

SECRETARY: Please don't declaim so. Give yourself up or you will bear the responsibility for a completely pointless bloodbath of German blood.

CAPTAIN: You have no German blood! You have surrendered to black and red filth. I will not surrender. Better to spill German blood than destroy the national rebirth! I am not afraid!

SECRETARY: I must point out to you that inflation is no longer rising. Give yourself up…

CAPTAIN: No!

SECRETARY: Should you obey, then I can tell you unofficially that I will do everything in my power to prevent you from being punished. Do you understand?

CAPTAIN: Punished? Punished? What for? For not allowing myself to be betrayed?!

SECRETARY: You're the sort of man whose position occasionally has to be made clear to him…

CAPTAIN: I refuse! I can see quite clearly! I know friend from foe!

(*Silence.*)

SECRETARY: I'll give you time to think.

CAPTAIN: Not necessary.

SECRETARY: If you do not hoist the white flag then we will open fire, however much pain it causes and however much we'd prefer not to. You must bear the responsibility for the fact that we have been forced to shoot at German men for the sake of the German fatherland.

CAPTAIN: I accept that responsibility.

SECRETARY: You will have to bear it. (*He exits with the two regular SOLDIERS.*)

(*Pause. An early morning wind is blowing.*)

CAPTAIN: Dogs. Nothing but dogs. The worst treachery is on our own playing field! Did you hear? The competent authority wants reconciliation.

HALEF: Yes, I heard.

CAPTAIN: Bloody dogs. Do you believe in peace, Halef? Now we can begin to exist! Us! Run to Salm and tell him to come straightaway with his…

HALEF: Salm and his sidekick Rübezahl disappeared as soon as they found that we were surrounded. Gone. Ran away.

CAPTAIN: Ran away!

HALEF: Did you hear what that black coat said about punishment?

CAPTAIN: Are you afraid?

HALEF: Yes, I'm afraid.

CAPTAIN: Then run away too, coward.

HALEF: Yes, sir! I'll disband myself. And if I were you, I'd do the same. (*He exits.*)

CAPTAIN: Keep your mouth shut! I'm not dead yet. I'll not disband myself till the worms have eaten me. I am still myself.

(*SOLDIERS of the so-called Black Army appear.*)

Soldiers! The national army is marching despite the cowardly whores of politicians who despise us. Regular regiments are kneeling before the filthy black and red flag – your own fellow citizens have surrounded us and are threatening to shoot us down if we do not beg for mercy. Anyone who surrenders cannot call himself a soldier.

They want to annihilate us! They mewl about peace with the enemy and want to ban us forever! They do not want us to exist, they want to stab us in the back for a second time. They are ashamed of the national revolution!

FIRST SOLDIER: (*Stepping forward.*) Captain, I'm a soldier. I fight the enemy. I hate this Republic but I will not fire at German soldiers.

CAPTAIN: Those aren't soldiers, they are excrement!

FIRST SOLDIER: They are German, just like us.

CAPTAIN: If they are German, then every red is a German.

SECOND SOLDIER: As he is! As he is!

(*Silence.*)

CAPTAIN: Who said that?

SECOND SOLDIER: (*Stepping forward.*) I did.

CAPTAIN: You dog, dog. (*He hits him in the chest so he falls back.*)

(*We hear artillery firing in the background.*)

THIRD SOLDIER: (*Walking up to the CAPTAIN and pushing him back.*) Captain! I surrender. I don't want to go on. I fought for four years, the war is over! Get it? They forced me to join you, your barons, or they'd have slaughtered my family! I piss on your revolution! I've had enough of war! I don't want to be buried. I want to decay amongst the living!

CAPTAIN: (*Pulling out his revolver.*) Back off, back off, this is mutiny! This is treachery!

THIRD SOLDIER: (*Knocking the revolver out of his hand and hitting him hard.*) That's for your mutiny! That's for your treachery!

CAPTAIN: (*Shouting.*) Guard! Guard!

THIRD SOLDIER: (*Hitting him again.*) There's your guard! Keep your guard!

SECOND SOLDIER: We're not dying for you!

FIRST SOLDIER: On the field of your own personal honour!

THIRD SOLDIER: Not on your private field of honour! Comrades! The white flag! The white flag!

(*Gunfire. The SOLDIERS flee. The CAPTAIN alone. SLADEK enters.*)

SLADEK: Captain. They've freed the prisoners. I think it's mutiny. They hit me. One in particular. They heard artillery fire. Captain, you're covered in blood.

CAPTAIN: (*Smiling blackly.*) So?

SLADEK: (*Looking up.*) What's that noise… And what… (*A grenade goes off nearby.*)

CAPTAIN: They are firing at us! They must hit me. Quick march, Sladek. They want me! Only me!

SLADEK: Me too!

CAPTAIN: Only me! Only me! Who are you? Who are the others? Nothing! Nothing! Dismiss, Sladek, quick march!

SLADEK: I am not afraid. Killings are plentiful in nature, that never changes. Something's coming again.

CAPTAIN: They're firing their artillery at me!

SLADEK: (*Pointing to the fort.*) Captain! Thc white flag! (*Regular SOLDIERS appear. The CAPTAIN laughs at the SOLDIERS. SLADEK puts his hands up and surrenders.*)

End of Act Two.

ACT THREE

Scene 8

The Court of Regeneration

The JUDGE (who is the same as the PARLIAMENTARY SECRETARY) is interrogating the prisoner FRANZ.

FRANZ: I protest against my arrest.
JUDGE: You admit to having written this article?
FRANZ: Yes.
JUDGE: In this article you maintain that a competent authority of the German Republic secretly recruited and trained soldiers, contravening our promises to the outside world, and that a so-called Black Army was built up under the command of a former captain. You write further, that in order to protect their very existence, those troops took the law into their own hands – you talk about kangaroo courts. You also dare to make an extraordinary claim that people were tortured to death to prevent exposure, and that included not only those perceived as traitors but also complete innocents. You 'reveal' that the captain finally became the prisoner of his own soldiers, in the main moral and spiritual inadequates, who were the ones really in command. You also touch on a particular crime, a demonstrably quite ordinary murder, namely the Sladek case. Unfortunately we have not yet been able to arrest this Sladek.
FRANZ: Unfortunately. Otherwise he would himself explain to you that this was no 'ordinary' murder but a so-called execution in the so-called interest of the so-called fatherland. He told me so himself whilst I was at the mercy of the lawless soldiers, who would have beaten me to death had not the entire Black Army been disbanded by the competent authority.
JUDGE: I warn you, for your own sake.

FRANZ: Thank you.

JUDGE: Your conclusion is that the competent authority apparently recognised the bankruptcy of the domestic plan and that is why they forced the Black Army to disband. And you tell some sort of fairytale about a battle with artillery.

FRANZ: It is no fairy tale.

JUDGE: There was no battle with artillery, there was only some ludicrous attempted putsch by a tiny group of right-wing extremists, a ridiculous gaggle of ultra-nationalistic communists!

FRANZ: That is not true. That was the army of the alleged national revolution. Those were reactionary mercenaries, who wanted to enslave and disempower their own people behind the mask of the national dictatorship!

JUDGE: There was no Black Army!

FRANZ: I myself was to be beaten to death because I wanted to save the Republic. Is it not grotesque that the judiciary of the Republic I sought to protect is sentencing me because I am warning them?

JUDGE: No, it is not grotesque.

FRANZ: I realise that you consider it just.

JUDGE: You have been arrested for a specific crime, that of attempted treason. Please note the 'attempted'. I'm warning you. Every single German citizen is duty bound to know what will damage the German Reich, even if we are not obliged to do so by the outside world. If anyone ignores this, then they are to be considered fantasists, a danger to the public and an enemy of the state. The health of the nation would force us to arrest him on the spot.

FRANZ: The health of the nation is also the health of the people. The old state only took care of its ruling class – and it collapsed. Now the old guard are ruling the rubble. They want to renovate a ruin and cement it with guns and laws. However the people are climbing over the rubble and building a house, a house without a façade from the good old times.

JUDGE: Are you a conscientious objector?

FRANZ: I would be happy if we had an international criminal code, which had the power to punish war in the same way as murder. I view the fact that there will be war anyway as without moral value but not as an excuse.

JUDGE: Unfortunately there is no longer a Wehrmacht. Sadly, *si vie pacem, para bellum* as it says in Latin. Do you understand Latin?

FRANZ: No.

JUDGE: It means: if you want peace, prepare for war.

FRANZ: (*Smiling.*) I understood that, even if I can't speak Latin.

(*Silence.*)

JUDGE: (*Clearing his throat.*) Your article can only damage us, especially as we are not armed. It is oil on the water of the most vile enemy propaganda. It is treason, because you are hindering the rebuilding of our country and because that article will cause those abroad to doubt our honest desire for honest rapprochement.

FRANZ: Who is assassinating the honest friend of reconciliation? It is for reasons of domestic policy that former criminals are worsening the already terrible situation of the people. My article is fighting against shy power-mongers for an honourable peace...

JUDGE: (*Interrupting him.*) There was no Black Army! All your assertions are out and out lies!

FRANZ: They were going to murder me! I will prove everything!

JUDGE: I'm warning you – as I said, for your own sake. You are accused of the crime of attempted treason, if however you can prove to me that there really was a Black Army, then you will be convicted of the crime of actual treason and will not get away with a prison sentence of less than several years.

FRANZ: Either way I will be convicted?

JUDGE: Either way.

FRANZ: There is no defence?

JUDGE: Not for those who have committed treason. (*Pause.*) Are you a conscientious objector? Or a communist?

FRANZ: Someone once said there was a flaw in my reasoning – I understood that but I drew the wrong conclusion. You know, with regards my pacifism, it's quite right that my reverence for the individual is exaggerated, despite all the misery I see around me. And belief in the sacrosanct nature of every living being led me into the labyrinth of betrayal. Because there are people who are so morally corrupt that the Lord himself has given up trying to save them. Even in the temple Jesus lashed about him without bothering to mention spiritual salvation. God himself could not convert these people. They deserve to be kicked out of the temple of mankind like rabid dogs. Those who peddle on holy ground deserve to be destroyed, those who are too far gone to even imagine there is another way – the captain was right, although he didn't know it at the time. The 'when all's said and done' has nothing to do with me.

JUDGE: So you're a terrorist?

FRANZ: I must be.

JUDGE: You're waging battle against the state.

FRANZ: Your state.

JUDGE: There is only one state, I tell you, and it knows how to protect itself. Even the worm turns when it's been trodden on.

Scene 9

A harbour in the North Sea

SLADEK is talking to TWO SAILORS on a quiet quayside. The sun has nearly gone down.

FIRST SAILOR: What? You want to sail to South America round the Cape of Good Hope?

SLADEK: I think so.

FIRST SAILOR: Round the Cape of Good Hope?

SLADEK: To Nicaragua.

SECOND SAILOR: In South America?

FIRST SAILOR: Central America, you camel! Central America!

SLADEK: So what? Could be.

SECOND SAILOR: And who is waiting for you in Nicaragua, mutt? Rich aunt? Rich uncle?

SLADEK: No one. I'll go anywhere. I don't care. As long as it's quickly. It's not nice here. I heard about Nicaragua and thought, yes, that's it, I'll go there. I liked the name, it's so foreign, so different to here. It's not at all nice here – here, for example, it's always foggy. I want to go far far away. That's all.

FIRST SAILOR: Who are you?

SLADEK: Me?

SECOND SAILOR: Yes, you.

SLADEK: Why?

FIRST SAILOR: Because I think I know you. Aren't you the bloke who was with that woman, the widow, the old bit who fell for her subtenant, but suddenly it was discovered that her daughter was with child… I only saw the gentleman subtenant once in passing, but I don't know, you, maybe…that was over in Triest.

SLADEK: No, that's a so-called error. I was never in Triest, I only asked if you would take me with you as something, anything, as if I was a crate – you are sailors after all. I can do a bit cooking. I wanted to be a waiter but I'll carry coal if needs be. Just to get away.

SECOND SAILOR: You pulled off a stunt?

SLADEK: What do you mean? Why?

FIRST SAILOR: What would we get for you?

SLADEK: For me? From whom?

FIRST SAILOR: The public prosecutor.

(*Silence.*)

SLADEK: I didn't do anything, even though a reward is often offered for innocent criminals – I'm not one of them. Many people, I believe, both innocent and guilty, are persecuted. There's nothing can be done, there's no other way of organising it. Why do I want to leave Europe? I suppose you could say for reasons of population policy. There's not enough room here – I always feel the need to open a window to let some fresh air in. It's stifling here.

(*In the distance the 'Internationale' is being played.*)

FIRST SAILOR: Did you hear that?

SECOND SAILOR: Yes.

SLADEK: Please take me with you – to Nicaragua.

SECOND SAILOR: We're not going to Nicaragua. We're not going anywhere.

SLADEK: But you're sailors?

FIRST SAILOR: We're jackasses.

SLADEK: Why's that?

FIRST SAILOR: We're waiting, just like you, for something to change. We'd row to Nicaragua, even via the Cape of Good Hope, if we had to, elephant. But today there's one hundred sailors to every skiff.

SLADEK: So, you've nothing to do either?

FIRST SAILOR: Because we're lazy, that's what some professor said recently.

SLADEK: He was wrong, we aren't lazy, we're just too many. That was my first original thought in this world. Wouldn't it be fine if we were twenty million people less.

FIRST SAILOR: We're only ten thousand too many, but those ten thousand feel like twenty million.

(*A tumult in the distance.*)

SLADEK: Someone's screaming.

SECOND SAILOR: There's no need for it all.

FIRST SAILOR: What then?

SECOND SAILOR: The army and the coppers clean up the street and anyone left is shot – but they still don't give him an amnesty.

SLADEK: Who?

FIRST SAILOR: You don't know?

SLADEK: Maybe.

SECOND SAILOR: They put him in prison because he proved there was a Black Army, which wanted to shoot us all down like mad dogs.

FIRST SAILOR: It was treason. Everyone said so.

SECOND SAILOR: I heard him speak once, about two years ago. He's a brave man.

FIRST SAILOR: He fell in love with eternal peace. I'm sure he's been converted now! He went on about Moscow, was against action, he wants to talk the Republic back to health.

SECOND SAILOR: A brave man.

(*In the distance a shot, screaming. The music stops.*)

FIRST SAILOR: The German people, as one in their desire to promote progress, choose Article forty-eight.

(*He exits quickly.*)

SLADEK: (*To SECOND SAILOR.*) Do you really know the German constitution?

SECOND SAILOR: Oh yes!

SLADEK: I'd like to read it sometime. Recently I've been a bit distant from power, I mean, it's quite right that everything is about power, yet one has to have a bit of peace and quiet occasionally, do you agree?

SECOND SAILOR: No. Far from it, you snake! Far from it.

(*He exits.*)

SLADEK: (*Alone.*) I've heard that before. I'm hungry.

(*Silence.*)

Did they just shoot someone? Probably. Now it's all over, the sea is still and vast and deep. Majestic, you could call it. I always thought the sea would be green, in fact it's grey. And I pictured harbours differently, more so-called romantic. I suppose it's not that dirty. Which is better, dying of hunger or thirst? Once there were some travellers in the desert who couldn't find water anywhere, so they drank their own blood till the very last drop – you'd have to be a camel to last longer. And yet there's more water on this planet than land. That's got to be wrong. There must be more land, that would be fairer because there really are too many of us. Now, what was the capital of Nicaragua?

(*Silence.*)

Nicaragua is bound to be beautiful. No winter there, only palm trees, everything just growing by itself. There's no

problem with hunger. I'd like to lie under a tree and not see a single house, but there must be a little stream nearby and then I'd say – it does exist.
(*Silence.*)
A steam ship. A great steam ship. Four storeys high, maybe even higher. All lit up, from top to bottom, it'll soon be on its way leaving a few behind. There'll be little sandwiches and famous women and society games. Not bad! And those dirty slags all done up doing nothing all day, nearly all American. You know, Sladek, if you died on the open sea, you'd be thrown into the depths with a wreath, that's general knowledge. And down there there's all sorts of fish, big and small, also general knowledge. One should be able to see through the sea, right down to fifteen thousand metres, that'd be something! Better still, if one could look through the earth! I don't believe the earth is round, I think it's flat, people just say it's round and then everyone copies everyone else. It can't be round, it's impossible.
(*He stares into the water. The sun goes down. KNORKE and HALEF arrive. SLADEK doesn't notice them.*)

HALEF: (*Under his breath.*) You swear he's coming? I bet you we'll wait to no purpose. He'll manage to give himself up, then somehow he'll end up happily signing everything that bastard wrote.

KNORKE: No, he won't. The Captain might be conceited, but, when all's said and done, he's also intelligent. He gave me his word he'd come. I sorted the passport and everything else. We have been shamefully betrayed. Although from a purely legal point of view those were murders – and the public prosecutor has no choice but to prosecute.

HALEF: I bet you his vanity will lead him straight to the scaffold.

KNORKE: We are all vain, but we are not all mad.

HALEF: The Captain is a fool.

KNORKE: All great men were fools, history taught that.

HALEF: A non-commissioned sergeant thinks he's a second Alexander the moment he's made an officer. I saw it immediately; he's not a great man, yet he's a fool. A drummer boy, not a general!

KNORKE: Salm's over there already. His brother-in-law is a farmer.

HALEF: Is it true that young Horst is dead?

KNORKE: Malaria.

HALEF: I heard that Rübezahl threw him overboard during the voyage.

KNORKE: Also possible.

(*Silence. It is now dark.*)

HALEF: It's about time he was here. I bet you he doesn't come.

(*The CAPTAIN appears.*)

CAPTAIN: (*Very quietly.*) I nearly broke my oath. It's so cowardly to creep away but in the end, no one can ask me to sacrifice myself for some bloody traitor, can they?

SLADEK: Captain.

KNORKE: What's that?

SLADEK: It's me.

KNORKE: What do you mean – 'me'.

SLADEK: Me. (*He approaches them.*) Captain. I recognised you immediately even though it is dark. (*He spots KNORKE and HALEF.*) You, too? Is this fate? Whatever it is, I don't mind, because you can help me, right? I've got to go away, to another world, although I didn't do anything and anything I did do was for the fatherland. I'm being followed like some common criminal and yet it was all about ideals. Hey, what's your problem?

KNORKE: What's your problem?

SLADEK: My problem? Wait a second. It's me, Sladek, comrades!

KNORKE: I am not your comrade!

CAPTAIN: I know you.

KNORKE: For God's sake, keep your mouth shut, you don't know him, steer clear!

CAPTAIN: I know you. You are the cowardly dog who was the first to surrender, I'll never forget your ugly mug!

SLADEK: No, you're wrong!

CAPTAIN: You're him. That face, that ugly, ugly face…

KNORKE: No, it's not him!

SLADEK: I'm someone else.

CAPTAIN: (*Kicking him hard.*) So take that for someone else! And that…!

SLADEK: (*Bending over double.*) Ow…!

KNORKE: They're all the same. Is he really worth hanging for?

HALEF: Someone's coming!

KNORKE: Let's go! We don't know any Sladek!

(*KNORKE exits quickly, followed by the CAPTAIN and HALEF.*)

SLADEK: (*Alone.*) We don't know any Sladek. We don't know any Sladek. If someone is mistaken for someone else, then that's bad. No one remembers him, or in this case, Sladek. Everything about him has been forgotten, once and for all, outside and in, as if he'd never been, and it's not just a matter of the individual Sladek, and yet… No, there's no point in thinking about it. I wish I could swim to Nicaragua. Why am I not a fish?

(*Pause.*)

Can fish see the little stars? I once heard that each fish is connected to a little star, but that's rubbish. I wonder which little star I was born under? It should be worked out and then children could only be born when there are good stars in the sky. Once the old card reader told me that in 1922 Poland would be destroyed, France half destroyed, Paris completely annihilated, whilst England would sink into the sea and Vesuvius would erupt again, terrible – and Germany would have a monarchy again and the Bavarian prince Rupprecht would be crowned Kaiser in Berlin. That should all have happened last year, I don't know, prophecies are ignored, although no doubt so-called seers do exist. Everything runs according to one specific rule, which is a pity. At first I thought life would be pointless without rules but now I know it's pointless anyway, and that's a bad rule.

(*A SUPERINTENDANT and two DETECTIVES appear. The SUPERINTENDANT is the same as the JUDGE.*)

SUPERINTENDANT: In the name of the law! Sladek, you're under arrest!

SLADEK: (*Mechanically.*) Me?

SUPERINTENDANT: You! Do not deny that you are Sladek, we know everything! I am arresting you for the murder of the widow, Anna Schramm.

SLADEK: At long last.

(*A DETECTIVE takes hold of him.*)

SUPERINTENDANT: Resistance is useless.

SLADEK: Gentlemen, I know.

Scene 10

The case of Sladek

The JUDGE, PUBLIC PROSECUTOR and BARRISTER sitting underneath a cross.

JUDGE: Name?

SLADEK: Sladek.

JUDGE: Date of birth?

SLADEK: Seventh of July 1902 in Hohenstein on the border.

JUDGE: Occupation?

SLADEK: I wanted to be a waiter.

JUDGE: Well?

SLADEK: No luck.

JUDGE: Instead you allowed yourself to be kept by the widow, Anna Schramm?

SLADEK: No.

JUDGE: What then?

SLADEK: She didn't just give me everything. It was a proper deal, we'd agreed on it, it only looked as if I was living off her. You see, I gave her something in return for everything she gave me.

PROSECUTOR: And what was that?

SLADEK: Myself.

(*Laughter is heard in the public gallery.*)

JUDGE: Accused, I'm warning you.

SLADEK: Why? What did I say?

JUDGE: Silence! Accused! Do you plead guilty to the crime?

SLADEK: It's all very complicated. It's very difficult to say anything because there is too much to say. It's quite true that Anna and I weren't getting along so well, that there were quite a few arguments, that it often came to so-called blows and even more often I'd take something from the cupboard and go and entertain strange women in public gardens. I admit that because I love righteousness, but I don't feel guilty. When I think back I realise it was all down to the difference in our ages. Gentlemen. When I first met Anna she was a good fifteen years younger than she was at the end, although only four years had gone by, but desire disappeared really after only two years, you know, the natural desire. Sirs, it's not really a problem as such, it's just sad.

BARRISTER: I request that the accused be examined by a medical practitioner to see if he is in his right mind.

PROSECUTOR: I move that my learned friend's request is turned down and that the accused is compelled in the strongest possible terms to behave in accordance with the dignity of the court.

SLADEK: Pardon?

JUDGE: Accused. You deny having murdered the widow Anna Schramm?

SLADEK: I absolutely deny it. I have never murdered anybody.

JUDGE: So you are saying that this murder was carried out by a so-called kangaroo court and was a criminal act by the so-called Black Army, who took the law into their own hands? Accused, nowadays we are able to discuss those confused times more openly, we can see them in a clearer light. And we thank God that we have overcome those terrible days of inflation. The German people are now enjoying a period of powerful growth, they withstood many terrible things and have succeeded in creating an economic wonder.

(*The public gallery is heard clapping.*)

SLADEK: Despite powerful growth and anything else, I can only say that I'm innocent, so to speak.
PROSECUTOR: 'So to speak'?
SLADEK: When all's said and done, yes. I have always said that killings are plentiful in nature and that never changes, but, gentlemen, I was against it. I'll never forget afterwards as I drove back to the headquarters with the four soldiers, it was dark and pouring with rain.
JUDGE: The four soldiers have disappeared.
SLADEK: All of them. I believe they're in Nicaragua.
PROSECUTOR: So you admit to appearing that night on the Prinzenstrasse with four soldiers and that these four soldiers murdered the widow, Anna Schramm.
SLADEK: Yes.
PROSECUTOR: And what were you thinking?
SLADEK: Me? Well, first I thought: she'll have to die.
PROSECUTOR: Thank you.
SLADEK: Not at all.
PROSECUTOR: That's enough.
SLADEK: No, that is not enough, because straight afterwards I changed my mind, but it was too late. I even shouted 'Stop!' because I thought about justice, and because of this 'Stop!' they nearly shot me, and I knew it was too late to change anything – yet, I still shouted 'Stop!' You see, there was no longer any need to kill her. She'd thought about it. She'd decided not to betray anyone. Whatever happened.
BARRISTER: What did she want to betray?
SLADEK: The Black Army.
JUDGE: I would like to point out that it is not necessary to go into the complexities of the so-called Black Army here as it is not relevant to the fate of the accused. Those men were not soldiers, they were confused, fanatical idealists who believed they were fighting for the fatherland. However in the case of Sladek here, one has to doubt whether in fact it was all about ideals…
SLADEK: Oho!
JUDGE: You will remain silent! Murder is murder and in every case, the murderer is personally culpable!

SLADEK: But I thought…

JUDGE: Quiet! You wanted to murder the widow, Anna Schramm, you've admitted to that. Now talk.

SLADEK: But what can I say? I've always thought for myself, but then everyone started saying that the individual didn't count, that he has to sacrifice himself for the greater good, whether he wants to or not. I heard that again and again until I finally believed it, and it is so, but at the same time it's wrong, because now I am to be done as an individual for something I did as part of the whole. As you can see, I have been wrestling with all these problems.
(*Laughter is heard in the public gallery.*)
Everything I didn't actually do but wanted to do, I did for the fatherland, it was all, so to speak, out of idealism. I would never have killed her if this fatherland had not existed, one could say I sacrificed myself in the end, but it just wasn't recognised. Without the fatherland there might only have been cross words between us, at most I'd have thumped her and then it would have been all over, just like in other relationships.

BARRISTER: The accused is the product of a sick time. A man who cannot remember our proud past, whose voice broke during our glory years and who began to think only after we lost the war, this speaks volumes. Without any sense of morality he denied everything that had to do with human feelings and brooded over a whole number of self-evident truths: he was concerned only with himself and with no sense of culture. I plead mitigating circumstances for a ghost: here sits the era of inflation.

SLADEK: Please view me as a man and not as an era.

BARRISTER: I request that the accused be examined by a medical practitioner to see if he is in his right mind.

JUDGE: The court will hear from witnesses.
(*FRANZ enters.*)

BARRISTER: I protest against the swearing in of this witness. Someone sentenced for treason is not fit…

JUDGE: No tirades, please!

PROSECUTOR: The witness declares under oath that the accused Sladek admitted murdering the widow, Anna Schramm.

FRANZ: Yes.

SLADEK: No.

JUDGE: Silence.

SLADEK: I didn't murder anyone!

FRANZ: I was nearly murdered myself by those animals. Do you dare to deny that you told me yourself that the pitiful woman was 'executed' in the supposed interest of the so-called fatherland.

SLADEK: That is true, but I never said that I killed her.

FRANZ: He lies! He lies!

(*Silence.*)

SLADEK: I know that you don't lie, so there must have been a misunderstanding.

FRANZ: I understood you.

SLADEK: No, I was misunderstood. Did I not say to you twice that I'm a so-called retiring man and that everything I say to you is for your ears only? You've forgotten that. I thought about everything you said to the Captain. You could say you converted me: when all's said and done, there is only Sladek. And now? What about here? In this courtroom?

FRANZ: (*Almost mocking him.*) And you could say you converted me: Sladek should not be considered at all because then the big picture will not move forwards. It doesn't matter how much I deceived myself, some individuals will always be destroyed.

SLADEK: To be sacrificed for the bigger picture – but what about Sladek?

FRANZ: I will no longer be held back, do you hear?

SLADEK: Yes.

FRANZ: You are not my concern.

SLADEK: Now you're lying.

FRANZ: You think so?

SLADEK: That's not very nice of you.

JUDGE: No private conversations! Accused! There is no point in denying it. Think of God.

PROSECUTOR: And God is watching you, Sladek!
SLADEK: No God is watching me. Gentlemen, what is God? Some old man with a long beard. And what does he see? Nothing. He sees nothing. He lives way up there, too far away to see anything but the bigger picture, you can see that because of the state of things down here. Gentlemen! My defence counsel was good enough to suggest that I might be a ghost – perhaps – but I would ask you to consider that I might be a so-called unborn ghost. Gentlemen! Perhaps I just need to catch up and then forget it all. Let's suppose I did murder someone, then I would ask you to release me anyway, perhaps something can be made of it, I'm even beginning to believe myself that I'm a so-called unborn ghost.
BARRISTER: I move that the accused be examined to see if he is in his right mind.
SLADEK: But…
PROSECUTOR: I propose a life sentence and stripping of all civilian rights.
SLADEK: Why?

Scene 11

A fairground

Wax figures, carousels, flea circus and acrobats. The sun is shining.

LOTTE: Summer's going to be good this year. I hope they finally manage to fly over the North Pole.
SECOND GIRL: The newspaper says the odds are seven to one in London.
THIRD GIRL: Forget the newspaper! Have you seen the man with a bosom and the legs of a camel – unbelievable. And there's a dwarf over there who's a hermaphrodite – and the bed of Haarmann, the mass murderer is displayed in the gallery.
LOTTE: No, not the Chamber of Horrors. I refuse. I can't stand wax figures. I'd rather have real criminals!

SECOND GIRL: (*Newspaper in hand.*) Have you seen, another one's escaped? A murderer, he was only in for two years – then he attacked a postman, who gave him everything and now he's wandering around free. It's the best thing – just hand everything over.

LOTTE: (*Looking in the newspaper.*) Doesn't look too bad to me.

SECOND GIRL: (*Newspaper in hand.*) Nothing special about his profile. There's a ten thousand mark reward for his capture.

THIRD GIRL: I wouldn't recognise him if I saw him.

LOTTE: There are too many escapees.

SECOND GIRL: (*Newspaper in hand.*) Three days ago it was a madman, and he's still not been caught. Someone like that is a danger to the public.

LOTTE: It's all so unreal.

(*SLADEK appears.*)

THIRD GIRL: (*Newspaper in hand.*) Have you seen, hat brims are getting wider. Hopefully the weather'll stay. It's been raining every Sunday and I didn't bring my coat with me.

LOTTE: Why aren't there any young men around any more? You have to make such an effort as a woman. A good thing I'm no longer a virgin.

SECOND GIRL: (*Newspaper in hand.*) I'd like to see that Haarmann's bed.

LOTTE: Go on then. I'll wait here. (*She accidentally bumps into SLADEK.*)

THIRD GIRL: We'll be straight back! (*She goes off with the SECOND GIRL.*)

LOTTE: I'll be here.

PALM READER: (*To SLADEK.*) Does the gentleman want his hand read? Past and future.

SLADEK: Thank you.

PALM READER: Looks as if that young lady is very interested in your future.

LOTTE: (*Saucily.*) Very interested indeed.

PALM READER: Are you listening?

SLADEK: Yes. How much is the future?

PALM READER: Just twenty pfennig.
SLADEK: Fine.
PALM READER: Over here then. Hmmmm, the past... don't close your hands.
SLADEK: No, I only want the future.
PALM READER: Without the past?
SLADEK: Yes, no past.
PALM READER: As you wish.
SLADEK: That is what I wish.
PALM READER: You come from a cultivated family – you're technical but with a strong creative bent – more architect than fine artist.
SLADEK: True.
PALM READER: You have a great connection to the sea, not too many cares, yet you suffer in your imagination...
SLADEK: Also true.
PALM READER: That's your artistic blood. Closed character, wary of women. A feeling for family.
(*LOTTE smiles. SLADEK is embarrassed.*)
As to the future. You're going away soon, that's quite clear. Far far away. Across the seas. Rich you'll never be – you're too sensitive for all that. However you will live well and live to be about eighty.
SLADEK: That'd be nice.
LOTTE: Of course.
PALM READER: Twenty pfennig please.
SLADEK: (*Paying her and staring at the shy LOTTE.*)
That would be nice. That would be very nice, if... Excuse me, if you would... Do you like going on the carousel? That would be very nice, Fräulein.
LOTTE: It might well be nice, but I have to wait for my friends, they'll be back any minute.
SLADEK: That's not so nice. It really would have been very nice indeed if we could go on the carousel together, or whatever: there's so much to see here, but it's not so interesting if you're on your own. I don't know anybody, you see.
LOTTE: You're a stranger here?

SLADEK: A complete stranger.
LOTTE: Are you English, perhaps?
SLADEK: That's right.
LOTTE: The newspapers say that in London the bets are on seven to one that they'll succeed in flying over the North Pole.
SLADEK: What? Who will?
LOTTE: You know, the North Pole.
SLADEK: The North Pole?
LOTTE: You must know it.
SLADEK: Fly over it?
LOTTE: You are peculiar.
SLADEK: Very peculiar. Yes, I am. It's a long time now since I read a newspaper, you could say I've not been well, but now it's beginning to come back. So they're going to fly over the North Pole are they?
LOTTE: I hope so.
SLADEK: So do I.
LOTTE: I think sportsmen are real heroes. They place their own lives at risk for the sake of progress. All radio stations are there to support them, I can't think about anything else.
SLADEK: You know, there are also sportsmen who sort of sacrificed themselves, perhaps not exactly for progress but for something else, and they certainly weren't supported by radio stations, that's right, and afterwards no one believed them...do you know what I am talking about?
LOTTE: No.
SLADEK: For example, during war time. And after.
LOTTE: You mean the world war?
SLADEK: Yes.
LOTTE: The day before yesterday I saw an amazing film about the war. It was really well directed. An American film.
SLADEK: So, an American film.
LOTTE: Always the best. It's through films like that that you get a really clear picture of what the war was like,

better than in books. Just look at that dancer on the tightrope! Wonderful!

SLADEK: It can't be easy, dancing on a tightrope.

LOTTE: Do you like dancing?

SLADEK: Not really. (*Pause.*) I can do lots of things. There was a time I thought I could do nothing, then I realised that I can do something.

(*The sun suddenly disappears.*)

LOTTE: Heavens, it's going to rain!

SLADEK: Quite likely.

(*The two other GIRLS come back at the run.*)

THIRD GIRL: You see, it's raining! This really isn't funny.

SECOND GIRL: It'll soon stop.

THIRD GIRL: (*Without a coat.*) No, it's bound to continue. Dress, shoes – why didn't I bring a coat with me?

LOTTE: We could go to the cinema.

SECOND GIRL: To see the American war film?

LOTTE: No, it was amazing but I don't need to see it a second time.

SECOND GIRL: Of course, that'd be boring.

GIRL: (*Without a coat.*) Now it's pouring. Why don't any of us have an umbrella!

(*The three GIRLS run off.*)

SLADEK: I've never had an umbrella. And this North Pole business…

(*It rains. A POLICEMAN appears, he is the same person as the JUDGE.*)

POLICEMAN: You're under arrest. You know why. You have been observed relieving yourself, not in the public convenience, but against the back wall of the flea circus. Why? It is strictly forbidden. You have defiled the flea circus. Your name?

SLADEK: What is the fine?

POLICEMAN: Five marks. What's your name?

SLADEK: It's a so-called long and difficult name, allegedly a foreign name, I am just about to leave, to travel a long way…

(*A ship's sirens go off.*)

POLICEMAN: Stop! Your pass. Your papers.

SLADEK: Here – but the ship is leaving any minute.
POLICEMAN: Which ship?
SLADEK: I can't pronounce the name.
POLICEMAN: (*Leafing through and then stopping short.*) Where are you going to?
SLADEK: To Nicaragua. I don't have a ticket. I'll work my passage.
(*Silence.*)
POLICEMAN: (*Still leafing through, very quietly.*) You received an amnesty.
SLADEK: A line was put underneath me. I hope there's nothing untoward. Tell me, is there a consulate in Nicaragua?
POLICEMAN: Of course.
SLADEK: That's good.
(*Silence.*)
POLICEMAN: (*Returning his papers.*) Everything's in order.
SLADEK: I won't relieve myself against the flea circus again.
POLICEMAN: It is expressly forbidden. (*He exits.*)
SLADEK: It really won't ever happen again.

The End.

A SEXUAL CONGRESS

Rund um den Kongress

Characters

FERDINAND

SCHMINKE

LUISE GIFT

THE GIRL

ALFRED

WAITER

SECRETARY-GENERAL

CAPTAIN

POLICEMAN

PRESIDENT

CHAIRWOMAN

MEDICAL ADVISOR

TEACHER

DELEGATES

MEMBER OF THE AUDIENCE

Scene 1

FERDINAND is standing on a street corner leaning on his walking cane. He is lost.

SCHMINKE meets him.

FERDINAND: Excuse me. I'm a stranger to these parts and don't know my way around. I'm looking for the Miramar restaurant, can you tell me where it is?
SCHMINKE: Restaurant?
FERDINAND: Miramar.
SCHMINKE: It's not a restaurant.
FERDINAND: A café perhaps?
SCHMINKE: No, it's a brothel.
FERDINAND: Interesting!
SCHMINKE: That too.
FERDINAND: Most peculiar. Actually, I wanted to meet my brother Alfred, who is a waiter in this Restaurant Miramar, and it will be three years in November since...
SCHMINKE: I never give out information about brothels – as a matter of principle.
FERDINAND: But I just want to see my brother Alfred.
SCHMINKE: As a matter of principle – no!
FERDINAND: 'As a matter of principle' – that tone. I know that tone. 'As a matter of principle' – your name is Schminke, isn't it?
SCHMINKE: You know me? From where?
FERDINAND: A matter of principle, Mr Schminke.
SCHMINKE: But who are you?
FERDINAND: I am me, Mr Schminke. Most peculiar. Yes, which leads me to something else: if you don't know who I am, then you will probably have forgotten my sister, too.
SCHMINKE: Who is your sister?
FERDINAND: My sister is dead.
SCHMINKE: This is outrageous!
FERDINAND: Outrageous. Outrageous!
(*Exit SCHMINKE.*)
That's one bad man.

(*Enter LUISE GIFT.*)

Excuse me. I'm a stranger to these parts and don't know my way around. Do you know a dance hall called Miramar?

LUISE: Dance hall? That's a good one.

FERDINAND: An establishment.

LUISE: A cattle market.

FERDINAND: A *maison de discretion.*

LUISE: Young man, young man!

FERDINAND: I have been informed that this Miramar is a somewhat discreet joint.

LUISE: You've been informed?

FERDINAND: Just now.

(*Silence.*)

LUISE: Does it have to be in the Miramar?

FERDINAND: You're too kind.

LUISE: Oh please! You won't regret it.

FERDINAND: Don't talk of the devil if you don't wish him to appear.

LUISE: Are you superstitious too?

FERDINAND: When it comes to my own person, yes.

LUISE: Sometimes I daren't even leave the house. Especially when there are flags everywhere.

FERDINAND: Apropos house. Where is this house?

LUISE: This particular house is nowhere in particular. It's burnt down.

FERDINAND: Burnt down?

LUISE: In April.

FERDINAND: My God!

LUISE: It was probably arson. All down to envy.

FERDINAND: Tell me: who was burnt down with it?

LUISE: Who did you have in mind?

FERDINAND: Actually, I wanted to visit my brother Alfred.

LUISE: Alfred? He's your brother?

FERDINAND: Do you know him?

LUISE: Unfortunately.

FERDINAND: Is he still alive?

LUISE: Unfortunately. He's a complete scoundrel.

FERDINAND: Still?

LUISE: He broke his word of honour.

FERDINAND: Most peculiar. What word of honour was that?

LUISE: He gave me his word of honour that he would not tell anyone that I had broken my word of honour. He does it to annoy me, everyone knows that everyone breaks their word of honour.

FERDINAND: I was ten when I first broke mine. I like to remember it, I get all melancholy. There's a sort of peace about remembering one's very first word of honour.

LUISE: I think you must be a good man.

FERDINAND: (*Tipping his hat.*) Thank you.

LUISE: My pleasure.

(*SCHMINKE returns and appears to be looking for something.*)

FERDINAND: Good evening, Mr Schminke!

SCHMINKE: (*Starting, he recognises FERDINAND and approaches him.*) Sir. You said a little while ago that I knew your dead sister. Who or what was your sister?

FERDINAND: A tart.

SCHMINKE: What are you trying to say?

FERDINAND: I had two sisters. The youngest died after eleven minutes, the oldest was a tart.

SCHMINKE: So, what did I have to do with your eleven-minute old sister?

FERDINAND: I didn't mean that both my sisters were tarts. With regards my dead eldest sister, the tart, the one you've forgotten – well, I just wanted to remind you, that you owe this dead tart about fifty-three marks, and as I am her only heir…

SCHMINKE: Sir! I have never had congress with a tart!

FERDINAND: I mean a non-physical kind of congress. You are a spiritual person. As for myself, I am not a spiritual person, but even spiritual people have to pay their debts.

SCHMINKE: I don't have any debts!

FERDINAND: Are you or are you not a journalist?

SCHMINKE: I am, but what's that got to do with it?

FERDINAND: And my sister, the dead tart, supplied you with material for a particularly long article.

SCHMINKE: Material? What about?

FERDINAND: About the fight against prostitution. You made full use of the material this dead tart supplied without paying her a penny.

SCHMINKE: I wasn't obliged to pay her.

FERDINAND: Legally, maybe not. But morally, certainly.

SCHMINKE: I am a definite moralist.

FERDINAND: Who is paid eighteen pfennigs a line. Without my sister you wouldn't have been able to write more than half a line. Which is fifty per cent. Which amounts to fifty three marks.

SCHMINKE: This has nothing to do with your tart, this is all about fighting prostitution. That and much more! It's about an idea.

FERDINAND: At eighteen pfennigs a line.

SCHMINKE: You've got to live in order to fight for an idea!

FERDINAND: That's not what I've heard.

SCHMINKE: Should I let myself be crucified?

FERDINAND: Am I the good Lord?

SCHMINKE: There is no good Lord! And that's that!

FERDINAND: Hm!

(*Exit SCHMINKE.*)

LUISE: Who on earth was that?

FERDINAND: A bad man.

LUISE: Why?

FERDINAND: Because he won't pay what he owes a dead tart.

LUISE: Why don't you leave the dead alone?

FERDINAND: There are no dead, at least not when it comes to fifty-three marks. We human beings have an immortal soul.

LUISE: (*Studying herself in the mirror, lipstick in hand.*) As do I. As do I.

(*She continues with her make up and powder and hums Chopin's 'Totenmarsch' whilst doing it: Suddenly.*)

Alfred is in Café Rump.

FERDINAND: Rump? Rump. Sounds respectable enough. Is Alfred a waiter in this Rump? Has he been made head barman?

LUISE: No. He plays billiards.

FERDINAND: So?

LUISE: And cards. And chess. Then he plays billiards again.

FERDINAND: Then what's he living off?

LUISE: He's living off me.

(*Silence.*)

FERDINAND: Most peculiar. Tell me, where is this Café Rump?

LUISE: Just keep to your right, or your left even.

FERDINAND: Thank you.

LUISE: My pleasure.

FERDINAND: Most peculiar.

LUISE: You can't possibly miss it.

FERDINAND: My compliments.

LUISE: May you live a long life.

FERDINAND: Your servant.

LUISE: Likewise.

FERDINAND: Goodnight!

LUISE: A good man.

FERDINAND: Goodbye.

LUISE: God speed!

(*Exit FERDINAND.*
LUISE waves after him.
The GIRL appears.)

You gave me a shock! I thought it was someone else.

GIRL: Who?

LUISE: I don't know.

GIRL: It's only me.

(*Silence.*)

LUISE: Well?

GIRL: I've thought it all through.

(*Silence.*)

Yes, you're quite right. I should get paid for it.

LUISE: At last!

GIRL: At last.

LUISE: I always said you were bright.

GIRL: And I always knew you were right, I just didn't want to say so. Now I can say it. I'm going to do exactly what you do.

LUISE: It gets easier and easier.

GIRL: Who says so?

LUISE: Coué. (*Silence.*) You know, there's one thing I don't quite buy. That you've never done it for money. I just don't buy it. You must have. Haven't you?

GIRL: I only did it once for money.

LUISE: When?

GIRL: The day before yesterday.

LUISE: Well?

GIRL: Twelve marks.

LUISE: Congratulations.

GIRL: Is that a lot?

LUISE: Enough.

GIRL: I thought it was about right.

LUISE: Child. Infant. Twelve marks is a Bentley. For twelve marks people want something elegant. You have to be somebody. Make an impression. Walk up and down.

(*The GIRL walks up and down.*)

Walk like that and two marks would be stretching it.

GIRL: I'm not being sold at market.

LUISE: My, your language is choice.

GIRL: That's probably because I've read so many novels.

LUISE: Too much reading is unhealthy.

GIRL: I knew someone once, who wrote novels. In a pretty log cabin.

LUISE: There are some very pretty log cabins around.

GIRL: With a lake nearby.

(*Silence.*)

LUISE: We'll make it nice and cosy. You'll move in with me, of course. For as long as you want.

(*Silence.*)

GIRL: Remember asking me how old I was? I said twenty-three, but I'll only be twenty-three next birthday. In September.

LUISE: Why are you telling me that now?

GIRL: Just wanted to.
(*Silence.*)
LUISE: I look younger. Don't I?
GIRL: Younger than me?
LUISE: No, younger than me.
GIRL: Of course.
(*Silence.*)
LUISE: I've taken a subscription out for the local newspaper. It's going to be really nice. When we don't feel well, we'll make some tea and stay at home, even if it is evening. What are you doing now?
GIRL: Nothing in particular.
LUISE: Then go over to my place, I'll be there soon. Have a look at the book on the chest of drawers. You need to know all that, particularly the second section. It's a medical work *Loving in the Natural World.* With appendix.
GIRL: I've seen it already.
LUISE: The appendix too? You've got to be careful there.
GIRL: Where are you off to?
LUISE: The doctor. (*She screeches suddenly.*) Don't look at me like that!
ALFRED: (*Appearing and studying the situation.*) Why do you always squeal? (*He paces up and down.*) Piano, Luise! Piano! She's gnashing her fangs again.
LUISE: I don't have fangs.
ALFRED: Of course you have fangs.
LUISE: I have teeth.
ALFRED: That's what they all say. Is that the girl?
LUISE: What girl?
ALFRED: The girl.
LUISE: Where?
ALFRED: There.
LUISE: There. There is no girl there.
ALFRED: So who is that?
LUISE: That is nothing.
(*Silence.*)
ALFRED: (*Approaching Luise.*) Luise, you're making me nervous. And that means you're not taking good care of yourself. It was only yesterday that you told me all

about a girl, who wanted some time to think it all through…

LUISE: (*Interrupting him.*) That girl has nothing to do with you.

ALFRED: Piano!

LUISE: That girl wants only me. No one else. Do you hear?

ALFRED: (*To the GIRL.*) Did you hear that, my dear?

GIRL: Yes.

ALFRED: Perhaps she's telling a porky?

(*The GIRL is silent.*)

LUISE: (*Approaching ALFRED, quietly.*) Leave her for me, please.

ALFRED: (*Mockingly.*) The 'nothing'?

LUISE: You gave me your word of honour…

ALFRED: (*Interrupting her.*) Introduce me to the girl.

LUISE: Animal.

ALFRED: Shush.

(*LUISE starts sobbing.*)

GIRL: Ugh! Calm down! That's disgusting!

ALFRED: You're telling me!

LUISE: (*Staring at the GIRL.*) What did you say?

ALFRED: *D* like dire, *i* like idiot, *s* like silly, *g* like girl, *u* like us, *s* like stupid, *t* like time, *i* like in, *n* like no, *g* like go.

LUISE: Disgusting.

GIRL: Yes.

ALFRED: Yes.

LUISE: Very disgusting?

GIRL: Very.

LUISE: Animal.

(*Silence.*)

ALFRED: (*To the GIRL.*) You're witnessing a sort of hysteria. Luise is sickly. Even as a child she suffered from a general porosity. Luise dear! Is your liver behaving itself? What did the doctor say?

LUISE: (*Beaten.*) I was just on my way to the doctor.

ALFRED: Well, off you go girl, quickly now. Health is everything. Fight the germs! Innoculate yourself!

You should take up sport.

(*The GIRL giggles.*)

One hundred metres. Discus. Hurdles. Pole vault!

LUISE: (*Expressionless.*) Show off. Show off.

ALFRED: (*Bowing before the GIRL and doing a little dance.*) *Voilà.*

(*The GIRL laughs.*)

LUISE: I'm going now. Yes. I'm going now.

(*She doesn't move.*)

ALFRED: (*To the GIRL.*) I'm Alfred.

GIRL: I thought so straightaway.

ALFRED: Why? Has she said unpleasant things about me?

GIRL: Quite the opposite.

ALFRED: My assessment of the situation thus far is that you have thought it all through.

GIRL: Yes.

LUISE: (*To the GIRL, apathetically.*) That's Alfred.

ALFRED: She's already had the pleasure.

LUISE: Alfred has to be mean, he can't help himself.

ALFRED: She's lying.

LUISE: (*Walking away slowly, then suddenly standing still.*) Alfred, I've just spoken to your brother.

ALFRED: My brother? Is he here? Since when?

LUISE: I bumped into him accidentally.

ALFRED: I'm only accidentally his brother, he's a complete fool.

LUISE: He's a good man.

ALFRED: Hanging around for a reason?

LUISE: I'm off.

ALFRED: Quick march.

(*Exit LUISE.*

Silence.)

Tell me, my dear, have you ever had your horoscope read?

GIRL: No. Do you know your way round the stars?

ALFRED: Well, I am interested in the occult. Luise, for instance, was born under the sign of positive Aquarius.

GIRL: What does that mean?

ALFRED: She has no soul.

GIRL: But she was very nice to me. She told me how to walk and all that. She's helping me. For one thing, she's letting me stay with her. (*Pause.*) Is she very ill?

ALFRED: She's likely to go blind.

GIRL: What's wrong with her?

ALFRED: Well, for one thing, she sleepwalks. That's right, when there's a full moon, she climbs out of the window, and down the drainpipe and dances the dance of her youth – the quadrille! She's quite grey in parts. You're blonde, aren't you?

GIRL: Who?

ALFRED: You.

GIRL: Blonde, yes.

ALFRED: A real blonde?

(*The GIRL takes off her hat.*)

Bravo! Bravo!

(*Silence.*)

Tell me, my dear, would you fancy earning five hundred marks a month?

GIRL: What?

ALFRED: Per month.

GIRL: Five…

ALFRED: Hundred. In cash. Guaranteed. You.

(*Silence.*)

GIRL: Thank you, but no thank you.

ALFRED: Are you completely stupid?

GIRL: Possibly.

ALFRED: You seem to be quite on the ball.

GIRL: I'm afraid.

ALFRED: Of me? How can you be afraid of me? I'm not even afraid of me!

(*Silence.*)

GIRL: What do I have to do to earn five hundred marks?

ALFRED: The usual.

GIRL: Who?

ALFRED: A certain Ibanez from Parana.

GIRL: Ibanez himself?

ALFRED: Not quite.

GIRL: I'm not going into a brothel.

ALFRED: There are no brothels in Parana! I have to tell you, that in this regard there are only apartments in Parana. One flat, one girl! That is the law in Parana. Helps avoid the shameless exploitation of young females and protect the respectable trade in girls. The Government of Parana…

GIRL: (*Interrupting him.*) Whereabouts is Parana?

ALFRED: In South America.

GIRL: No.

(*Silence.*)

Nononononono…

ALFRED: Do you love Europe so much?

GIRL: I'm not going to the colonies.

ALFRED: Terrible geography. It is a fact that there are only sovereign states in South America, apart from the colonies of British, French and Dutch Guyana. Free democratic republics. The population is mainly Spanish and Portuguese, average height, passionate and black. Which is why blondes are the thing.

(*LUISE appears.*)

Back from the doctor's already?

LUISE: I wasn't at the doctor's. I was listening.

(*Silence.*)

ALFRED: Goodbye, my dear! (*He exits.*)

(*Silence.*)

GIRL: Perhaps I will go to South America.

LUISE: Don't be spiteful.

GIRL: I'm not being spiteful.

LUISE: Nobody ever comes back from South America.

GIRL: Maybe I'll stay there then.

LUISE: You're staying with me.

GIRL: I'm not so sure I want to.

LUISE: And I'm not sure of anything! (*She approaches her.*) I'm not usually like this, but then I rarely get the chance.

(*She strokes her hair and then suddenly grabs it.*)

GIRL: Ow! Let me go!

(*She pulls away and hits her on the chest, so that LUISE falls back.*)

Leave me be! (*She runs away.*)

LUISE: (*Laughing.*) Goodbye! Goodbye! (*She listens out for a response.*)
(*Silence.*)
(*She shouts.*) Goodbye! (*She listens out again.*)
(*Silence.*
She whimpers.)

Scene 2

FERDINAND enters Café Rump, stops by the billiard table and looks around. He is the only guest.

The WAITER enters, chewing on a piece of bread.

FERDINAND: Good evening.
WAITER: *Bon appetit.*
FERDINAND: Excuse me. I'm a stranger to these parts and don't know my way around. Is this Café Rump?
WAITER: Yes.
FERDINAND: So why does it say 'Café Victoria' outside?
WAITER: Because it's called Café Victoria.
FERDINAND: Is the owner called Rump, perhaps?
WAITER: No. The previous owner.
(*Silence.*)
FERDINAND: Most peculiar. Has Herr Rump been dead a long time?
WAITER: Herr Rump is not dead at all. Herr Rump did not get probation.
FERDINAND: And what was he charged under?
WAITER: Paragraph one-eight-one, A. 'A male personage, who lives, whether partially or entirely, by exploitation of the immoral earnings of a female personage, working as a prostitute; or, who offers a female personage protection in order that she may carry out prostitution either sporadically or regularly, will be punished...'
FERDINAND: '...by imprisonment...'
WAITER: '...of no less than...'
FERDINAND: '...one month.'
WAITER: And since then, we've been called Victoria.
(*Silence.*)

FERDINAND: But why Victoria?
WAITER: You won't get it out of me that way.
FERDINAND: I was only curious.
WAITER: Why?
FERDINAND: Compassion. We are only human, after all.
WAITER: After all. Please sit down.

(*FERDINAND sits down.*)

What would you like? Coffee, tea, chocolate.

FERDINAND: Coffee.
WAITER: Cup or cafetière?
FERDINAND: Cup.

(*Exit the WAITER.*

ALFRED enters and notes FERDINAND, who does not see him. He takes his jacket off and plays billiards against himself in his shirt sleeves.

FERDINAND spots ALFRED and jumps up, surprised.

ALFRED looks at him for a moment, and then continues playing.)

Alfred!

ALFRED: (*Unmoved.*) What?
FERDINAND: You're not in the least surprised, that I surprised you!
ALFRED: No.
FERDINAND: Most peculiar.
ALFRED: I already knew.
FERDINAND: How?
ALFRED: You won't get it out of me that way.
FERDINAND: I was only curious.
ALFRED: Why?

(*FERDINAND sits down.*

Silence.)

WAITER: (*Bringing FERDINAND's cup. To ALFRED.*) Halleluja!
ALFRED: Coffee.
WAITER: Cup or cafetière?
ALFRED: Cafetière.

(*The WAITER exits.*

Silence.)

FERDINAND: Apparently you enjoy playing billiards. Very much?
ALFRED: Yes.
(*Silence.*)
FERDINAND: Alfred, what did I ever do to you?
ALFRED: Nothing.
FERDINAND: So?
ALFRED: So.
FERDINAND: I never did anything...
ALFRED: Precisely!
FERDINAND: So so.
ALFRED: Yes yes.
(*Silence.*)
FERDINAND: Most peculiar. I thought you'd be over the moon.
ALFRED: Because you happen to be my brother?
FERDINAND: Nevertheless.
ALFRED: I'm not concerned with family values.
FERDINAND: Quite right, we're a depraved family. You only have to think back – when I took my first holy communion, Father had just stolen the furs. Even Grandfather had previous convictions.
ALFRED: And Mother?
FERDINAND: Leave Mother out of it. She gave birth to us and that was enough.
ALFRED: True.
(*Silence.*)
FERDINAND: Even if I wasn't your brother, I'd've been happy if you'd been happier. It's only human.
ALFRED: Well if you've come for money, I'm sorry to inform you that I'm flat broke.
FERDINAND: You never were very kind.
ALFRED: I'm broke.
FERDINAND: I'm sorry about that. It's only human.
ALFRED: Do shut up. (*Silence.*)
FERDINAND: I, on the other hand, have made my way to the top. By accident.
ALFRED: (*Paying attention.*) By what?

FERDINAND: By accident.
ALFRED: Does this accident have a name?
FERDINAND: In fact, the good Lord himself helped me.
ALFRED: What exactly do you mean by the 'good Lord'?
FERDINAND: Two thousand marks.
ALFRED: (*Approaching him.*) What was that?
FERDINAND: (*Smiling.*) Yes.
WAITER: (*Bringing ALFRED's cafetière of coffee.*) Where do you want it?
ALFRED: There – here. (*He sits down next to FERDINAND.*) (*The WAITER puts the cafetière and starts to play billiards in a desultory fashion.*)
And, tell me: what are you going to use your good Lord for?
FERDINAND: Private income.
ALFRED: You could double your good Lord.
FERDINAND: Oh!
ALFRED: Double it. Guaranteed.
FERDINAND: Who would guarantee it?
ALFRED: Me.
FERDINAND: That's not my kind of business.
ALFRED: It's an above-board kind of business.
FERDINAND: Back to the guarantee.
ALFRED: Straightaway! Firstly, I have an agency.
An employment bureau for South America. If one only possessed a small portion of your good Lord, one could make the business considerably more profitable.
FERDINAND: What sort of employment.
ALFRED: On the whole, nursery nurses.
FERDINAND: Have you no shame? Do you think I'm that stupid?
ALFRED: Pardon me, I thought you were even more stupid. (*Silence.*)
FERDINAND: Nevertheless, I might still consider the transaction, even though from a purely human point of view it is not responsible, but even the human being is not absolute and that is why there have to be concessions. As you can see, I have developed an interest in philosophy.

ALFRED: I can see that.

FERDINAND: For instance, at this moment I'm drinking a cup of coffee. If I could double the good Lord, we'd be talking about a cafetière. For human beings, life often revolves round a cafetière.

ALFRED: I can see that.

FERDINAND: I have learnt a lot from life and would have nothing against being able to order a cafetière of coffee.

ALFRED: You could be talking about a coffee plantation...

FERDINAND: (*Interrupting him.*) Go on!

ALFRED: I am at this very moment about to close a deal. With the renowned company Ibanez. In Parana. Unfortunately, I'm only able to cover half the transport costs; if one could pay for the entire journey now, your good Lord would double within six weeks.

FERDINAND: And the guarantee?

ALFRED: Still me.

FERDINAND: That's too risky.

ALFRED: But you are my brother.

FERDINAND: I am not concerned with family values.

ALFRED: Don't parrot me. Even if we weren't brothers – it's only human.

FERDINAND: Don't parrot me.

(*Silence.*)

ALFRED: Risk nothing – and you double nothing.

FERDINAND: I'm not a gambler.

ALFRED: But what about your cafetière?

FERDINAND: That might be a reason.

ALFRED: To take a risk.

FERDINAND: A bold move!

ALFRED: A magnificent manoeuvre!

FERDINAND: Monte Carlo!

ALFRED: Or bust! Deal?

FERDINAND: Deal.

(*LUISE enters.*)

Good evening, dear lady!

LUISE: Good evening.

(*ALFRED spots her and flinches. He gets up.*)

Please come here.

ALFRED: (*Approaching her.*) Well?
LUISE: Do you know what I really want to do right now?
ALFRED: No. And what's more, I don't care.
LUISE: Yet again, you've broken your word.
ALFRED: I'm not interested, Luise dear.
LUISE: You're a corrupt creature.
WAITER: (*To LUISE.*) And what would the lady like?
ALFRED: Nothing.
LUISE: Coffee.
WAITER: Cup or cafetière?
LUISE: Cafetière.
(*The WAITER exits.*)
ALFRED: Well then, *adieu*!
LUISE: Stop! Did you or did you not give me your word of honour that you'd leave me the girl? That you would not take her from me, like the others…
ALFRED: (*Interrupting.*) I'm a salesman. Heart and soul.
LUISE: If that girl boards a ship for South America…
ALFRED: (*Interrupting.*) Then what?
LUISE: (*Smirking.*) Theoretically speaking.
ALFRED: I did not like that finger pointing.
LUISE: And he once swore an oath for you…
ALFRED: Back off now. Do I ever mention your past?
LUISE: In my interest? Never.
ALFRED: And do I emphasise the sergeant? Do I ever mention, that I was once the great hope of the European film industry?
LUISE: (*Grinning.*) A *bon viveur*…
ALFRED: I will not allow my name to be dragged through the mud. That was a long time ago. You know that my eyes couldn't bear the klieg lights, right?
LUISE: Right.
ALFRED: Luise dear. What will happen if the girl decides to go to South America?
LUISE: (*Grinning.*) Prison. Prison.
ALFRED: For you?
LUISE: For you.
ALFRED: Luise dear. You once committed perjury. For a perfectly good reason.

LUISE: For you.

ALFRED: Doesn't matter.

LUISE: Nothing matters to me.

ALFRED: To me, neither. Don't forget that.

LUISE: Oh, I know that. That's why I'm going to report you…

ALFRED: Not so loud…

LUISE: Or what?

ALFRED: You take care. Nothing can happen to me, because you've no second witness.

LUISE: (*Grinning.*) Oh, how the law always protects you…

ALFRED: Justice does exist, after all.

LUISE: There are people who don't care about second witnesses…

ALFRED: Utopians. Idealists. Anything but political realists.

FERDINAND: Please introduce me to the lady.

ALFRED: My brother Ferdinand – Frau Luise Gift.

FERDINAND: (*Bowing.*) I have already had the pleasure.

LUISE: We have met.

FERDINAND: Delighted.

LUISE: Since we last saw each other, your brother Alfred has broken his word of honour yet again.

ALFRED: (*To LUISE.*) Mortally wounded.

LUISE: Don't you touch me. Don't you touch me…

ALFRED: Marvellous. I really cannot imagine what company you've been keeping that makes you think I might maltreat a woman.

LUISE: You've never laid a finger on me?

ALFRED: Never.

LUISE: What about March the seventeenth?

ALFRED: (*To FERDINAND.*) She's lying.

(*FERDINAND smiles, embarrassed.*)

LUISE: Animal.

ALFRED: Back off now. (*He exits.*)

(*The WAITER returns and puts LUISE's cafetière on FERDINAND's table.*)

FERDINAND: (*To LUISE.*) Please do join me.

(*The sound of drums in the distance.*
LUISE freezes.
SCHMINKE rushes into the café and sits down.)

WAITER: (*To SCHMINKE.*) What can I bring you?

SCHMINKE: Coffee.

WAITER: Cup or cafetière?

SCHMINKE: Cup.

(*He pulls a manuscript out of his pocket and starts correcting it.*
FERDINAND recognises SCHMINKE.
The sound of drums. Suddenly there are flags everywhere, Café Rump is bedecked with huge flags. Military music. Cheers and enthusiastic applause in a packed hall.
The WAITER listens carefully. FERDINAND stares at SCHMINKE.
Silence.)

LUISE: (*Nervously approaching the WAITER, horrified. She babbles.*) Doctor. It's really scaring me, doctor…

WAITER: I'm not a doctor.

LUISE: Did I say doctor?

WAITER: You should take better care.

LUISE: What? Tell me, why are there suddenly so many flags everywhere? I'm so afraid of these flags because, then there are so many flags in the mirror, and then I notice, that I am soon to… (*She falters.*)

WAITER: To…

LUISE: Just four weeks ago I could read from here: 'For Ladies' and 'For Gentlemen'. Now it's all blurred. I can't see anything clearly. As time goes on, everything gets blurred. Doesn't it?

WAITER: Probably.

LUISE: How easy that is to say. Now I'm going to write a postcard.

WAITER: Is that so?

LUISE: (*Is somewhere else.*) Postal greetings. To myself.

FERDINAND: Excuse me, I'm a stranger to these parts and don't know my way around. Why are there suddenly so many flags everywhere?

WAITER: To honour the Congress.

(*Enthusiastic applause is heard again.*)

FERDINAND: What sort of Congress?
WAITER: An international Congress.
LUISE: (*Furtively.*) And what does the Congress want?
WAITER: It wants to organise the international fight against prostitution. With particular emphasis on the international white slave trade.
(*LUISE sits down.*
The WAITER puts a little upright flag on the table.)
According to an edict from the whole cabinet and in accordance with instructions from the local police, flags must be hung everywhere. Non-accordance is a punishable offence.
LUISE: (*Grinning madly.*) Hoist the flags! Hoist the flags!
WAITER: Quiet! (*He listens.*) If you listen very hard, you can hear what the Congress is saying, but you have to have a very good ear.
(*Silence.*)
Now the reporter is talking.
LUISE: What's he saying, the reporter?
WAITER: I don't know. He's speaking Spanish.
FERDINAND: That's Portuguese.
WAITER: Do you speak Portuguese?
FERDINAND: No.
LUISE: So, they want to fight prostitution…
WAITER: In the Congo as well as in Berlin.
FERDINAND: As well as in Chile.
WAITER: As well as in Columbia.
FERDINAND: As well as in Ecuador.
WAITER: As well as in Paraguay.
FERDINAND: As well as in Uruguay.
WAITER: As well as in Venezuela.
FERDINAND: As well as in San Salvador.
SCHMINKE: Where's my coffee?
WAITER: Cup or cafetière?
SCHMINKE: Cup!
LUISE: Who's that?
WAITER: A bad man?
FERDINAND: Have you forgotten, Madam? That's the man who owes a dead tart fifty-three marks.

LUISE: And what does this bad man want?
WAITER: A cup of coffee.
FERDINAND: So he can fight the oldest profession.
LUISE: I see, he's a delegate. (*She gets up.*)
WAITER: From Sumatra.
FERDINAND: From Java.
WAITER: From Parana! From Parana!

(*LUISE sits down at SCHMINKE's table and smiles.*
SCHMINKE moves to another table.
FERDINAND and the WAITER look on interested.
LUISE sits down by SCHMINKE and glances at his manuscript.)

SCHMINKE: What do you want?
LUISE: (*Smiling.*) You have to write more clearly, otherwise it's unreadable. You want to combat the white slave trade?
SCHMINKE: I am amazed at your perception.
LUISE: I beg you! Sir! A girl is about to be sold to South America!
SCHMINKE: I am sorry to inform you that I am not interested in individual cases. As a matter of principle.
FERDINAND: A matter of principle.
SCHMINKE: To enter into the minutiae of individual cases simply causes pointless distraction.
LUISE: So, you don't want to distract yourself and would prefer that the girl is sold…
SCHMINKE: (*Interrupting her.*) I am not a policeman! Report it to them.
LUISE: I don't have a second witness.
SCHMINKE: Even if you did have a second witness you could not, I am convinced, change the substance of these matters. It makes no difference at all whether the girl prostitutes herself in South America or Central Europe. The white slave trade plays a secondary role, the primary one is prostitution and above all, its origins. (*Silence.*)
LUISE: So, you're combating the oldest profession as a matter of principle, young man?
SCHMINKE: Yes, if that's fine by you.

LUISE: (*Grinning.*) It's fine by me, go ahead, fight me, lover boy…

SCHMINKE: (*To the WAITER.*) Where on earth is my coffee?

WAITER: Cup or cafetière?

SCHMINKE: A cup! A cup, for the hundredth time!

WAITER: Naughty naughty! (*Exits.*)

FERDINAND: A bad man.

LUISE: Naughty naughty – and may one ask: what is your chosen weapon? Your mighty pen, perhaps?

SCHMINKE: Unfortunately.

LUISE: (*Spikily.*) Maybe you want to become president one day?

SCHMINKE: I would ask you to bear in mind, that I am correcting a memorandum. To be addressed to the Congress.

LUISE: (*Imitating him.*) I would ask you to bear in mind, that your Congress is about to combat me.

SCHMINKE: Not you! Only your profession!

LUISE: Only? And what am I supposed to do, once your Congress has got rid of my profession, hm? What can I do? I will have to start again at the bottom. (*She imitates him again.*) I would ask you to bear in mind, that the delegates all want to destroy me! Correct your memorandum and persuade the Congress to punish the hotels that make such a profit from us!

SCHMINKE: (*Stands up.*) You have completely misunderstood the…

LUISE: It's a scandal, it is! A scandal!

(*The WAITER appears with SCHMINKE's cup of coffee.*)

SCHMINKE: I'll pay now.

WAITER: Fifty-three marks.

LUISE: You should be ashamed of yourself! You should be ashamed! Stealing from a dead tart!

FERDINAND: It's a matter of principle.

Scene 3

SCHMINKE is in the square waiting in front of the Congress hall. The square is full of flags.

Excited applause is coming from inside the Congress hall.

SCHMINKE listens: walks up and down.

The SECRETARY-GENERAL appears. He is in tails and looking very nervous.

SECRETARY-GENERAL: Herr Schminke!
(*SCHMINKE hurries up to him.*)
Are you Herr Schminke? I am the Secretary-General of the International Congress for the International Fight against International Prostitution and have a tremendous amount to do. It is indeed most regrettable that you were overlooked when it came to sending out press passes, as both I and my colleagues attach particular importance to healthy relations with the press. In any case, I am delighted to be able to inform you, that the self-sacrificing efforts of the Congress have led to considerable success. Already today, the first day, the Congress has put in place twelve sub-committees, which will ascertain the running order of the points to be discussed. Oh yes!

SCHMINKE: I am more than delighted, that the running order of the points to be discussed can be determined on the first day.

SECRETARY-GENERAL: Should be determined. Oh yes!

SCHMINKE: And with regards the non-arrival of my press pass, I would in fact have been most surprised if I had not been overlooked.

SECRETARY-GENERAL: Oh yes!

SCHMINKE: And with regards the fight against prostitution...

SECRETARY-GENERAL: (*Interrupting him.*) Oh yes! So, that's it. Excellent. (*He tries to leave.*)

SCHMINKE: Stop! This is not just a matter of a press pass!

SECRETARY-GENERAL: What then?
(*SCHMINKE approaches him with his manuscript.*)
What's that?
SCHMINKE: A memorandum.
SECRETARY-GENERAL: And what has it to do with me?
SCHMINKE: It's to be addressed to the Congress.
SECRETARY-GENERAL: Title?
SCHMINKE: 'By removing the bourgeois stranglehold on society, the resultant official and unofficial prostitution will disappear.'
SECRETARY-GENERAL: Who says so?
SCHMINKE: You know who.
(*Silence.*)
SECRETARY-GENERAL: I don't know anything. And you should leave the bourgeois stranglehold alone, you Communist. Oh yes!
SCHMINKE: Do you dare to deny that prostitution is solely the product of economic necessity?
SECRETARY-GENERAL: Not solely!
SCHMINKE: Ninety-nine per cent!
SECRETARY-GENERAL: Ninety-eight!
SCHMINKE: Ninety-nine!
SECRETARY-GENERAL: One hundred! If you also want to take spiritual poverty into account! Even princesses suffer! And there is also suffering to be found on the golf course! Oh yes!
SCHMINKE: Don't get so carried away.
SECRETARY-GENERAL: I am fully aware that certain elements mock every sign of spiritual poverty as bourgeois prejudice. Oh yes! So: I confirm herewith receipt of your so-called memorandum, which the Congress will simply put away on file. Why? Because it is well known that the oldest profession is precisely that. It is indestructible, because the principle of the oldest profession is anchored too deep inside us, in fact, one could almost say, it is part of the make-up of a human being. Oh yes!
SCHMINKE: You are defending prostitution?

SECRETARY-GENERAL: You force me to! Oh yes!
SCHMINKE: Oh no.
SECRETARY-GENERAL: Don't you try and distract me, sir!
SCHMINKE: So what is the point of the Congress?
SECRETARY-GENERAL: Organisation! To organise the international fight against international prostitution – internationally. Oh yes! (*He tries to leave hurriedly, but stops suddenly, turns around and stares at SCHMINKE.*) What did you just say?
SCHMINKE: Subversion.
SECRETARY-GENERAL: I'm warning you.
SCHMINKE: Thank you.
SECRETARY-GENERAL: My pleasure. I'm warning you for the second time. The Congress disputes your moral right to subvert it and your political right contravenes the constitution. I'm warning you now for the third time. If you do not leave this square immediately, I will have you removed. Oh yes!
(*SCHMINKE does not move.*)
So, are you going to step back in line voluntarily?
SCHMINKE: Is that how you treat all your volunteers?
SECRETARY-GENERAL: My cup of forbearance is running out. I'm warning you – for the fourth time.
SCHMINKE: The fifth time.
SECRETARY-GENERAL: The sixth time! I'm only counting up to ten. On ten you will face a firing squad. Guaranteed. The Congress might be good, but it is also strict and consequently just. Oh yes! (*He counts.*) Seven. Eight. Nine. Well?
SCHMINKE: Ten.
SECRETARY-GENERAL: Be quiet! Who's counting here? Who is counting, in the truest sense of the word?! Me or you?!
SCHMINKE: Ten.
SECRETARY-GENERAL: Will you shut up, you fanatic! Oh that would be just marvellous if you become a martyr! The Congress doesn't want any shining halos. I personally wouldn't harm the hair on a flea's head. When all's said and done I'm just an employee who

makes a living by being seen to take responsibility for the Congress. What about a compromise?

SCHMINKE: I'm counting.

SECRETARY-GENERAL: Herr Schminke. I'm the head of a family and if you do not leave this square, the very first thing they'll do is fire me.

SCHMINKE: I want to see if the Congress has the courage to stand me up against the wall on the count of ten.

SECRETARY-GENERAL: Of course the Congress has the courage, but I have to bear the responsibility, you irresponsible idiot! You of course will take absolutely no responsibility for being shot! 'Not the murderer, but the murdered is guilty' another literary invention! Oh yes!

SCHMINKE: (*Counting.*) – Seven, eight, nine, ten!

(*Roll of drums.*

The SECRETARY-GENERAL puts his hands over his ears in despair.

SOLDIERS with gas masks and bayonets appear in the background.)

SECRETARY-GENERAL: What a mess! Here's the brass with extra knobs on.

CAPTAIN: (*Stepping forward and speaking with a strong Welsh accent.*) Please, forgive me. But I was certain I heard someone counting to ten – oh, good day to you, Secretary-General sir. And what's the Congress up to now? Passing on advice? Yes or no? Apropos Congress: Henrietta's getting a divorce. And Henrietta's sister is Josephine. And Josephine's sister is that Polly!

SCHMINKE: Captain! It was I who counted to ten, and I demand to be executed.

(*Silence.*)

CAPTAIN: (*Staring at SCHMINKE, suddenly speaking as a Guard's officer.*) What? Why? Who is this Turk?

SECRETARY-GENERAL: He is fighting against the bourgeois stranglehold on society.

CAPTAIN: (*Welsh.*) The bourgeois stranglehold on society! Devil only knows what that is. Apropos bourgeois stranglehold: Christa is going to marry a Jew.

SCHMINKE: Why don't you get on with it?

CAPTAIN: (*Guard's voice.*) Shut your trap, you little devil! Turk!

SCHMINKE: I demand to be executed!

CAPTAIN: (*Guard's voice.*) Be quiet! Be quiet!! No one gives orders around here, around here people obey orders. Discipline. Turk!

SECRETARY-GENERAL: My name is Pontius Pilate and I wash my hands in innocence. My name is mole – I am blind, I see nothing. The sole person responsible for any riot damage or acts of God is that Turk over there! Oh yes!

CAPTAIN: (*Welsh.*) But Herr Mole sir, nobody gives a damn who's responsible.
(*He gives the order.*) Troops halt!
(*The SOLDIERS come to a standstill.*)
Now. Do you want to observe the execution, Herr Mole sir, or not?

SECRETARY-GENERAL: Thank you, but no thank you. I can't watch executions, my stomach is predisposed to nerves.

CAPTAIN: (*Welsh.*) You can't be that soft, Herr Mole? Or are you telling me you're against the death penalty?

SECRETARY-GENERAL: Oh no!

CAPTAIN: (*Welsh.*) You know that a delinquent like that is just a poor sod, but we have to put him out of his misery or else how do we stay in control? It has to be like this, in the name of the Father!

SECRETARY-GENERAL: Amen! (*He exits at speed.*)

CAPTAIN: (*Giving orders.*) To prayer!
(*The SOLDIERS pray.*
SCHMINKE stands with his back to the audience as if against an imaginary wall.)
Present arms!
Aim!
Fire!
(*The SOLDIERS fire at SCHMINKE.*
There is tremendous applause from the Congress Hall.
SCHMINKE stays upright without moving a hair.)

CAPTAIN: Left turn! Quick *march!*

(*The SOLDIERS exeunt.*

The CAPTAIN lights a cigarette.

From a small bourgeois apartment we can hear the 'Blue Danube Waltz' (piano and violin).

The CAPTAIN hums along.)

SCHMINKE: (*Approaching him.*) Captain.

CAPTAIN: Sorry. To whom do I have the honour?

SCHMINKE: You just executed me.

CAPTAIN: (*Welsh.*) Aha, Sir Schminke. But of course, you were just executed. Although, to tell the truth, Sir Schminke, once I've done my bit, the whole thing's over and done with. You've been punished for your part and if someone has atoned for their misdeed, then as far as I am concerned, it's been dealt with. I don't bear grudges. It's as if I had nothing against you. Would you like a cigarette…? (*He offers him one.*)

SCHMINKE: You are mistaken. I am dead.

CAPTAIN: (*Staring at him hard.*) I see. Yes. Anything you say.

SCHMINKE: I would ask you to bear in mind that you might have been able to get rid of me, but you cannot kill my ideas.

CAPTAIN: (*Welsh.*) Ideas? What sort of ideas would they be?

SCHMINKE: Are you afraid?

CAPTAIN: (*Welsh.*) Get away with you?

SCHMINKE: I am not a man, I am an idea.

CAPTAIN: (*Welsh.*) You might be surprised to learn that I'm not afraid of ideas.

SCHMINKE: There was once a Roman Captain, who said 'That is not how men die'. And what he meant was…

CAPTAIN: (*Interrupting him.*) And what did he mean, the Roman captain?

SCHMINKE: That he was looking to the New World.

CAPTAIN: America?

SCHMINKE: No.

(*Silence.*)

CAPTAIN: (*Understanding suddenly.*) I see.

SCHMINKE: Right.

(*Silence.*)

Goodbye. (*He exits.*)

CAPTAIN: (*To the audience. Welsh.*) You see, the New World, that was the Catholics, and the old, well that was the Jews, or, more precisely, the ancients. They were well... you've only got to think of the excesses of the Roman women. (*He thinks.*) But he didn't have to pension her off, that old Roman captain, even if the general decline, well certainly, visions of...Oh well. We should talk about something else.

Scene 4

FERDINAND is waiting in the harbour, whence the ships leave for South America. All the ships are covered in flags. He is standing underneath a banner 'Welcome to the International Congress for the International Fight against the International White Slave Trade'.

A POLICEMAN arrives.

FERDINAND: Excuse me, I'm a stranger to these parts and don't know my way around. Is it seven o'clock already?

POLICEMAN: When that siren over there goes off, you know it's seven.

FERDINAND: Where?

POLICEMAN: (*Pointing upwards.*) There.

(*Silence.*)

FERDINAND: I can't see any siren.

POLICEMAN: I can see it clear as daylight.

FERDINAND: I'm short-sighted, you see.

POLICEMAN: I'm not.

(*The siren sounds. Silence.*)

Now it's seven.

FERDINAND: (*Bowing.*) Thank you.

POLICEMAN: (*Saluting.*) My pleasure! (*He exits.*)

FERDINAND: (*Watching him go.*) A good man.

(*ALFRED enters, and greets him briefly and soundlessly. So FERDINAND returns the greeting soundlessly. Silence.*)

ALFRED: (*Suspiciously.*) Wasn't that a policeman?
FERDINAND: Possibly.
ALFRED: What did he want from you?
FERDINAND: Nothing. I wanted something from him.
ALFRED: Don't debase yourself.
FERDINAND: I only asked if it was seven already…
ALFRED: I'm on time.
FERDINAND: So am I.
ALFRED: Do you have it with you?
FERDINAND: Yes, yes. (*He smiles coyly.*)
ALFRED: (*Staring at him.*) The whole good Lord?
FERDINAND: (*Embarrassed.*) Yes. No. I was just thinking, that perhaps to start off with, half of my good Lord could, would, should, surely be enough.

(*Silence.*)

ALFRED: Idiot.
FERDINAND: Pardon?
ALFRED: Hand it over.

(*FERDINAND gives him half of his good Lord.*
ALFRED counts the notes then puts them in his pocket and gives him a receipt.)

There! (*He breathes a sigh of relief.*) Space to breathe. The competition throttles you if you're a small merchant, but even with just half a good Lord in your pocket, it's possible to found a proper going concern. (*He ruminates.*) Touch wood!

FERDINAND: Good luck!
ALFRED: Shush.

(*Silence.*)

FERDINAND: So what does that make me?
ALFRED: My shareholder. My co-director. A member of the board!

(*He proffers his hand.*)

FERDINAND: (*Shaking it.*) Alfred!
ALFRED: Touch wood!
FERDINAND: To our success!
ALFRED: Shush! I'm superstitious.
FERDINAND: But surely congratulations are…

ALFRED: (*Having just spotted the banner, he stares at it fascinated and reads it out.*) ...International Congress... fight against...white slave trade...welcome. Welcome?

FERDINAND: Yes.

ALFRED: What's that all about?

FERDINAND: That's the Congress.

ALFRED: That is embarrassing. And with luck, not an omen. The very day I expand my business. Welcome? ...Well, the Congress can't harm us, however, yet, nevertheless, despite all that, maybe...

FERDINAND: When do I get my cafetière?

ALFRED: What cafetière?

FERDINAND: My cafetière of coffee? That's the only reason I got involved. Everything I do, I do just for a cafetière.

ALFRED: And I am related to that.

FERDINAND: You can't help it.

ALFRED: Idiot.

FERDINAND: Pardon?

(*Silence.*)

ALFRED: (*Quietly.*) I can't stand you any longer.

FERDINAND: Pardon?

ALFRED: (*Loudly.*) Go to the Café Rump and order a cafetière of coffee – on me.

FERDINAND: (*Staring at him, distressed.*) Please forgive me, dear brother.

ALFRED: What now?

FERDINAND: For believing that you were worse than you are. I would never have thought that you had so much heart. Thank you. I will never forget it. (*He is about to exit, then stops.*) Sorry. I'm a stranger to these parts and don't know my way around. What is the best way from here to Café Rump?

ALFRED: You're following it.

FERDINAND: Goodbye. (*He exits.*)

(*ALFRED looks at his watch and starts to leave.*
LUISE appears and blocks his path.
ALFRED stares at her, without saying hello.
Silence.)

LUISE: Don't laugh at me, please.

ALFRED: (*Grinning.*) You cripple. You misshape. (*Harshly.*) Out of my way! I have a rendezvous.

LUISE: With the girl?

ALFRED: Maybe.

LUISE: The girl, she went from me.

ALFRED: (*Impatiently.*) Went from you...?

LUISE: Well, went from my mind.

ALFRED: (*Pricking up his ears.*) Really?

(*LUISE nods – yes.*)

Congratulations. (*He glances at his watch and heads off.*)

LUISE: Alfred! I just want a minute of your time.

ALFRED: A minute is sixty seconds. Sixty is a lot. (*He yells at her.*) And lighten up a bit, will you?

LUISE: I'll put on a smile as soon as I'm sure you'll forgive me...

ALFRED: For that scene earlier? The threat without the second witness? For God's sake, I'm not that petty.

LUISE: Hit me.

(*Silence.*

ALFRED studies her suspiciously and goes up close.)

Hit me.

ALFRED: No.

LUISE: Don't torture me, hit me.

ALFRED: Why?

LUISE: Because I betrayed you. I said that you sold the girl to South America – hit me.

ALFRED: (*Slowly, menacingly.*) To whom did you betray me?

LUISE: The Congress.

ALFRED: So?

LUISE: First I told a delegate, but he didn't want to know, because he was so principled – and then I looked for the girl everywhere and found her nowhere and then I'd had enough...(*She shouts.*) Up here, in my head, I'd had enough...(*She whimpers.*) So I went to the Congress and told it all to the Secretary-General.

ALFRED: And what did the Secretary-General say to it all?

LUISE: He was very polite, the Secretary-General, and escorted me to the door and then said that without witnesses one couldn't really do anything, but that he would possibly take up the case...in one form or another...

(*Silence.*

ALFRED pinches her arm.)

Ow! Ow! Ow...

(*Silence.*)

ALFRED: That was perfidious.

LUISE: I take it all back. I recant.

ALFRED: Hyena.

LUISE: Please forgive me. Please.

ALFRED: I won't hit you.

LUISE: Please hit me in the face. Punch me.

ALFRED: Left or right?

LUISE: Right in the middle...please...

(*Silence.*)

ALFRED: Your breath smells. Of schnapps.

LUISE: I'll make it up to you.

ALFRED: But can you unmake it? No, as Strindberg, would say.

LUISE: Please. Else I'll be so alone.

ALFRED: I won't.

LUISE: Don't lie. And don't laugh at me, please.

(*Silence.*)

ALFRED: Let's not become emotional. Let us not hurt each other. Let's dissolve this liaison, which brought us much real happiness, gently and properly, so that we can look back and remember without a nasty taste in the mouth. Look, Luise dear, I am young and you are old. You can't force a young man, who's still growing and developing, to manacle himself to you forever. There's no point in forgiving you, because then, on the one hand, you will only cause more trouble and on the other, you're no good to me any more. You see, the good Lord himself has helped me. Do you understand?

LUISE: No. No, I don't understand. Don't poke fun at me...

ALFRED: You just look so funny. (*He exits.*)

LUISE: (*Alone.*) Gone.
(*Silence.*)
He was even polite. Gone – for good.
(*Silence.*)
What did he say? The good Lord helped him? If the good Lord exists – what have you got up your sleeve for me, Lord? Are you listening? You know I was born in Düsseldorf. What have you got up your sleeve for me...?
(*In the distance a jazz band is playing, it comes closer, the harbour turns into Café Rump: the guests, mainly prostitutes, tipsters and pimps, are being served by the WAITER. A new banner goes up: 'Dance in Café Rump. Swing with the mood.'*
The jazz band goes up on stage.
LUISE is as if she is dreaming it all. People start dancing.)

POLICEMAN: (*Coming up out of the floor and raising his hand.*) Stop!
(*Everyone comes to a halt.*
The WAITER bows to the POLICEMAN.
The POLICEMAN snorts.)
Table flags. Somewhere in here I know there's a flag missing – a flag in honour of the Congress.

WAITER: All flags are present and correct.

POLICEMAN: One is missing – and it is that one, third table from the left against the wall on the right opposite – that lady over there. (*He points jerkily to LUISE.*)

LUISE: (*Wailing.*) No! No! It's not my fault!

POLICEMAN: That's what they all say! Without exception!

LUISE: But I'm innocent, constable! I'm not responsible for the flag! I never hurt a single flag...(*She whimpers.*)

POLICEMAN: Heard it all before! Heard it all before! (*He gets his little black book out.*) Name?

WAITER: Constable! You can see it with your own eyes. If you would care to follow me please...

POLICEMAN: (*Rushing over to the specified table and stops suddenly.*) Hmm. The table has a flag on it. The flag is even fluttering in the prescribed direction, however...

WAITER: (*Interrupting him, shouting.*) So what do you want? What do you want?

POLICEMAN: Coffee. (*He sits down at the little table.*) For the time being.

WAITER: Cup or cafetière?

POLICEMAN: (*Unpleasantly.*) I'd watch your mouth, if I were you.

WAITER: So you want a cafetière?

POLICEMAN: Of course a cafetière – what else?!

(*The WAITER goes off.*

Everyone is dancing in Café Rump.

The GIRL appears and speaks to the WAITER.

LUISE recognises her and listens in.)

GIRL: Do you know Herr Alfred?

WAITER: Herr Alfred should be here by now. What do you want? Coffee, tea, chocolate…

GIRL: Coffee.

WAITER: Cup or cafetière?

GIRL: Whatever. (*She catches sight of LUISE.*)

LUISE: Herr Alfred should be here by now.

GIRL: Leave me alone!

LUISE: (*To the WAITER – tonelessly.*) Schnapps.

WAITER: What?

LUISE: (*Tonelessly.*) Schnapps. Your cheapest schnapps. (*She takes her head in her hands and sways.*)

WAITER: Are you not well, your ladyship?

LUISE: (*Burping.*) Maybe, your lordship…Everything is spinning, as if I'd drunk too much schnapps…it was a very cheap schnapps…the cheapest there is. (*She burps again and approaches the GIRL, tottering.*) Now it's all over. For good.

GIRL: I'm glad.

LUISE: Don't be cruel, please.

GIRL: I'm glad for you.

LUISE: That's nice of you. (*She burps, listen, burps again.*) Can you hear me?

GIRL: It's the schnapps.

LUISE: The cheapest schnapps. To forget my woes, all my woes…one day you'll understand…

GIRL: No I won't.

LUISE: Nor will I. I don't want to ruin it for you, perhaps you will find happiness in South America. I hope so.

GIRL: Please, don't stare at me.

LUISE: I wrote a poem yesterday. I can write poetry you know. When I'm alone I jot down poems. I've got it here. (*She unfolds a piece of paper and reads.*) 'So I search and search for you, you, my soul, my better self.' That's the poem.

GIRL: It's very short.

LUISE: But romantic. Take it with you across the sea. Across the romantic sea. (*She burps.*) And don't lose it. (*The GIRL puts the piece of paper away.*)
When are you leaving?

GIRL: The only one who knows that is Alfred.

LUISE: And his good Lord. (*Pause.*) *Bon voyage!*

GIRL: Thank you.

LUISE: (*Turning to leave, then turning back to the GIRL again.*) I wanted to ask – where did you sleep last night?

GIRL: Why?

LUISE: I just want to walk past.

GIRL: I earned twelve marks.

LUISE: Twelve? When I was your age I earned that much too. Well, the equivalent of, everything was much cheaper then. Am I very ugly?

GIRL: No.

(*LUISE burps and exits.*
Dancing in Café Rump.)

ALFRED: (*Entering the Café, he spots the GIRL, and takes her with him to a corner, i.e. at the front of the stage.*) Passport is fine. Ditto the ticket. Lower deck, tomorrow morning.

GIRL: (*Looking in the passport.*) What am I? Nursery nurse?

ALFRED: Careful! We're being watched.

GIRL: I wanted to be a nursery nurse, just for once.

ALFRED: When you're over there, send my greetings to Herr Ibanez and please also send my very best wishes to his charming wife.

GIRL: Is Herr Ibanez married?

ALFRED: Very much so. He doesn't do anything without his wife. She brought two Parisian brothels into the marriage and he only has usufruct.

GIRL: And what does he look like, this Herr Ibanez?

ALFRED: He could be a secretary-general.

(*The SECRETARY-GENERAL enters the Café Rump.*)

WAITER: What can I get you? Coffee, tea, chocolate…?

SECRETARY-GENERAL: I am looking for a certain Herr Alfred.

WAITER: What do you want from him?

SECRETARY-GENERAL: I will tell him that myself.

WAITER: I don't know a certain Herr Alfred.

SECRETARY-GENERAL: Don't deny it! I know everything! Oh yes!

ALFRED: (*Coming forward.*) And what do you know? And who are you? I am that certain person.

SECRETARY-GENERAL: I am the Secretary-General of the International Congress for the International Fight against the International White Slave Trade…

ALFRED: (*Interrupting him.*) There are no white slave traders!

SECRETARY-GENERAL: Oh no?

ALFRED: What do you know about it?

SECRETARY-GENERAL: Please don't get me wrong! My intentions are not hostile. After all, I'm merely a speaker for civilised nations. The Congress has just come to a unanimous decision, that men and women who work within the field of prostitution will be consulted about the nature of prostitution, in order to fight prostitution more effectively. Therefore, in the name of the Congress, you are called upon to cooperate with this lofty aim.

ALFRED: Is it really necessary?

SECRETARY-GENERAL: You don't need to be suspicious. The Congress wishes simply to appeal to the specialist in you. The Congress knows that a girl is to be sold to South America and the Congress, using me as their spokesman, wishes to have the opportunity to question this girl. The eight sub-committees have suddenly come to a majority decision and are interested in the psychological side. The purely human side, so to speak. It might simply be of academic value…

ALFRED: That girl is leaving in six hours.

SECRETARY-GENERAL: Then I request you send that girl to appear before the Congress immediately. There is a banquet on the programme, but between the courses there should be…

ALFRED: Do I have your word?

SECRETARY-GENERAL: Of course. Oh yes!

(*Pause.*)

ALFRED: If that girl should miss the crossing…

SECRETARY-GENERAL: You will be reimbursed for your losses.

ALFRED: One hundred per cent of my losses?

SECRETARY-GENERAL: Of course. Oh yes!

(*Pause.*)

ALFRED: What will you pay me for letting the girl appear before the Congress?

SECRETARY-GENERAL: I beg your pardon! We are only talking about information here…

ALFRED: Doesn't matter! Who is educated for free? I won't go under fifty marks.

SECRETARY-GENERAL: Forty marks.

ALFRED: Fifty.

SECRETARY-GENERAL: Forty-five.

ALFRED: Fifty.

SECRETARY-GENERAL: Forty-eight.

ALFRED: You should be ashamed of yourself.

SECRETARY-GENERAL: The Congress has to make savings and that is why I'm not ashamed. I am a civil servant.

ALFRED: A careful man.

SECRETARY-GENERAL: Forty-eight.

ALFRED: Please put it on record that I donate the two marks to the Congress. For the rehabilitation of fallen girls.

SECRETARY-GENERAL: On behalf of the Congress, I thank you for your generous donation. (*He smirks, bows and exits.*)

FERDINAND: (*Entering the Café Rump, he sits down and taps his walking stick on the table. Joyfully.*) Coffee! Coffee! Coffee!

WAITER: Cup or cafetière?
FERDINAND: A cafetière! And Herr Alfred is paying!
WAITER: Anyone could just come in and say that.
FERDINAND: Herr Alfred is my brother, sir!
WAITER: (*To ALFRED.*) Alfred! Is this really your brother?
(*The GIRL spots FERDINAND, screams loudly and reels backwards.*
Everyone is silent.)
FERDINAND: (*Jumping up and staring at the GIRL.*) No, what a coincidence, what a coincidence…
(*Silence.*)
ALFRED: Do you know each other?
FERDINAND: Certainly.
ALFRED: How do you know each other?
GIRL: (*Having pulled herself together.*) It's just a bit of a shock, that's all.
FERDINAND: Is that the girl we've sold to South America?
ALFRED: *Mais oui.*
FERDINAND: Most peculiar?
ALFRED: Why's that?
FERDINAND: Because that girl was once my wife.
(*The GIRL runs off. ALFRED runs after her.*
FERDINAND watches them, sits down mechanically and sips at his coffee.
Fanfare.)

Scene 5

The Congress at the banquet with discreet background music – Mozart.

Eating and drinking and making merry.

SECRETARY-GENERAL: (*Standing up somewhat nervously.*) Most venerable President! It is with deep reverence, simple human pride and profound gratitude that we are able, in the name of those that follow, to sound the drum and celebrate the extraordinary contribution made by this Congress. Oh yes!
(*A LACKEY drops a bowl, which smashes on the floor.*

The Congress jumps nervously.)

The unselfish nature of our work is the best weapon with which to fight for the permanent triumph of our ideals, the triumph of the spiritual over the corporeal…

DELEGATE: (*With full mouth.*) Bravo! Bravo!

ANOTHER DELEGATE: Hear! Hear!

SECRETARY-GENERAL: …the dominance of purified love and the irreversible eradication of purchasable lust. Oh yes! And so I stand here and raise my glass, in the name of the Congress, to the spiritual well-being of our revered President, the Director-General of the Association of the artificial oil works, the truly secret privy councillor, Dr Dr *honoris causae*!

CONGRESS: Bravo!! Three cheers.!!

(*Eating, drinking and making merry.*)

DELEGATE: What is the President called?

ANOTHER DELEGATE: *Honoris causae.*

DELEGATE: Is that Romanesque?

ANOTHER DELEGATE: He's a sound German.

PRESIDENT: (*Standing up.*) My Congress. May I be permitted to thank you for your trust, rarely given so freely, and to welcome a representative from the Ministry of War who is also here with us today.

(*The CAPTAIN, who is taking part in the banquet as the representative, gets up and bows slightly.*)

DELEGATE: Hurrah!

PRESIDENT: Let us hope for active support from the participating department. As I am convinced that by the next war we will have made considerable strides forward. Thank you, ladies and gentlemen!

(*The Congress rises to its feet, drinks a toast and sits down.*
Eating drinking and making merry.
A LACKEY enters and hands the SECRETARY-GENERAL a telegram. He opens its, reads it and turns pale.
The Congress watches him expectantly.)

SECRETARY-GENERAL: Sadly, God the all-powerful in his unfathomable wisdom has decided to allow the Secretary for Social Security of all people to have a heart attack. Oh yes! (*He sits down.*)

DELEGATE: Excuse me, could I bother you for the vegetables…

ANOTHER DELEGATE: Please!

DELEGATE: Thank you!

(*Eating, drinking and making merry.*)

THIRD DELEGATE: Yes, best to take some cream and roast the onions – do you know the dish?

DELEGATE: You know, I'm a layman when it comes to the physical training of the young.

FOURTH DELEGATE: How interesting! How interesting!

FIRST DELEGATE: If I could bother you for the vegetables?

FIFTH DELEGATE: Such a view of the world is what I like to hear. Nietzsche once said…

SIXTH DELEGATE: But why? Just because?

DELEGATE: Precisely! Precisely!

SLIGHT DEAF DELEGATE: For instance, I'm hard of hearing.

SHORT-SIGHTED DELEGATE: And I, for instance, am short-sighted.

THIRD DELEGATE: What! No! Mayonnaise? Mayonnaise? Impossible.

SECOND DELEGATE: Have you heard the one about two cyclists who meet on a road?

OLD-FASHIONED DELEGATE: Father, I call upon you!

FOURTH DELEGATE: Do you know how much property is going up in value?

SIXTH DELEGATE: No, no, I'm not anti-Semitic.

FIRST DELEGATE: Nevertheless. If I could bother you for the vegetables?

THIRD DELEGATE: My father was Commanding General.

OLD-FASHIONED DELEGATE: Really! Where?

THIRD DELEGATE: In Lucerne.

(*The GIRL appears before the Congress.*
The Congress stares at her bemused.
Pause.)

GIRL: I was eight years old when my father died, my mother was still alive. But we didn't want to have anything to do with each other as she couldn't stand my father. Very soon I had to start earning, because there was nothing, but in those early years I wasn't very happy, because I was treated very nastily. I learnt to sew. (*Pause.*)

PRESIDENT: What is this? Who is this person?

SECRETARY-GENERAL: Pardon me. Ladies and gentlemen, you seem to have forgotten, this person is the girl who has been sold to South America.

PRESIDENT: Of course, of course…

SECRETARY-GENERAL: According to a decision made by the eight sub-committees…

DELEGATE: (*Interrupting him and standing up.*) I am chairwoman for the eight committees. We decided unanimously to study this person, in order to help us combat prostitution from a spiritual point of view.

PRESIDENT: Of course, of course…

CHAIRWOMAN: We would like to ask this person three questions. First: did she let herself be sold willingly or was she forced into it; two, if she went willingly, then why; third, if she was forced, then why?

SECRETARY-GENERAL: So, Fraülein, we await your response. Oh yes.

GIRL: I am a nursery nurse.

CHAIRWOMAN: No more, I beg you, you are amongst friends.

SECRETARY-GENERAL: Were you forced to be a nursery nurse?

(*The GIRL is silent.*)

Yes or no?

(*The GIRL is silent.*)

Let us have your answer, please! Oh yes!

GIRL: I thought it all through.

SECRETARY-GENERAL: Be careful now! Did a certain Herr Alfred perhaps force you…

ALFRED: (*Suddenly appearing before the Congress.*) Stop! I will not be placed under suspicion. Please, Fraülein, tell the Congress: did I force you or did you not come to me? Tell them, please!

GIRL: I came to you.
ALFRED: There you are!
SECRETARY-GENERAL: Beg your pardon, sir, but we so often hear rumours…
ALFRED: There is no white slave trade. There are simply employment consultants. The rumours of girls being dragged somewhere against their will is simply rubbish!
DELEGATE: (*Standing up.*) Pardon me, but that might well be right.
ALFRED: You can bet your life.
DELEGATE: I am a medical advisor in Santa Fe de Bogota. Based upon my own wealth of personal experience I view the original cause of prostitution to be a certain degeneracy.
ALFRED: Well, what do you expect!
MEDICAL ADVISOR: A certain degeneration. Above all in certain specific muscles.
ALFRED: What else! (*He lights a cigarette.*)
MEDICAL ADVISOR: In Bogota the weather is usually beautiful. (*He stares off into the distance.*)
PRESIDENT: (*Laughing at a joke told by his neighbour.*) What? And then he said she had…
HIS NEIGHBOUR: Do you know the one about two cyclists meeting on the road…(*He whispers.*)
ALFRED: Tell us, sir, in your experience would you say that exports to Santa Fe de Bogota are worthwhile?
MEDICAL ADVISOR: Certainly! I know every single brothel in my homeland and thus I can advise you to export with a clear conscience. It is a sad fact that such business is always good capital investment.
ALFRED: Hm. (*He starts doing sums in his notebook.*)
MEDICAL ADVISOR: My dear fellow Congress members! It is my conviction that if we are talking about potential exports to my homeland, then we are not talking about forced exports. We are all after all human and we all have free will. I repeat: it is merely a sign of degeneracy. (*He sits down, eats and drinks.*)
ALFRED: Merely. (*He starts adding up on his fingers mid-air.*) Merely.

(*SCHMINKE appears.*
The SECRETARY-GENERAL stands up quickly and stares at him.)

SCHMINKE: (*To ALFRED.*) Merely? Don't lie. Don't you lie.

ALFRED: (*Not seeing him, his fingers still in the air.*) Did somebody say something?

SCHMINKE: Here it is not a matter of degeneration.

ALFRED: Rather?

SCHMINKE: Rather it is a matter of economic necessity.

ALFRED: Of course. But a businessman has to reckon on economic necessity. And pressing need. Where would we be otherwise?

GIRL: (*To ALFRED.*) Who are you talking to?

SCHMINKE: To me.

(*The GIRL stares at him anxiously.*)

ALFRED: I could have sworn somebody said something, something really stupid. (*He continues adding up.*)

SCHMINKE: (*To the GIRL.*) Fraülein, do you not find it unusual that I am talking to you and yet principles don't come into the equation. I know you. This is not about you personally.

(*The GIRL looks down shyly.*)

Personally, I don't want anything from you.

GIRL: You talk like a book.

SCHMINKE: Imagine you were a book and existed in millions of copies. Your German edition would have had to be reprinted more than a hundred times. I know that book. I know the readers and I know the publishers.

GIRL: I don't understand.

SCHMINKE: I know what you want and also know, what you have to do.

SECRETARY-GENERAL: (*Having pulled himself together, he shouts at SCHMINKE.*) Out! Get out! Immediately!

SCHMINKE: You're making a fool of yourself!

SECRETARY-GENERAL: I am not in the habit of making a fool of myself. You! Get out now! Now! Or I'll…

SCHMINKE: (*Interrupting him.*) Or what? Anyone who threatens me, I just laugh at them. You forget, I've already paid the price. Here before you stands an idea,

Secretary-General! And let me tell you: even if the Fraülein is degenerate, she nevertheless sold herself because of the yoke of economic necessity, as a result of the...!

(*The SECRETARY-GENERAL wipes the sweat from his brow and sits down exhausted.*)

PRESIDENT: (*TO THE SECRETARY-GENERAL.*) Don't you feel well?

SECRETARY-GENERAL: Just at the moment I...

PRESIDENT: Probably that business yesterday.

SECRETARY-GENERAL: Yes.

CHAIRWOMAN: What sort of a business was that?

MEDICAL ADVISOR: Our dear colleague was attacked by a murdering thief.

CAPTAIN: Even the firing squad had to be called into action.

CHAIRWOMAN: Aha.

SCHMINKE: It wasn't a murdering thief.

SECRETARY-GENERAL: Silent. Be silent. Oh yes!

PRESIDENT: Who are you talking to?

SECRETARY-GENERAL: Him over there.

PRESIDENT: (*Looking right at SCHMINKE.*) Where?

SECRETARY-GENERAL: Can't you see him?

PRESIDENT: I can't see anything.

MEDICAL ADVISOR: (*To the SECRETARY-GENERAL.*) I think you have been working too hard – may I take your pulse – (*He takes his pulse.*) Yes, you are sacrificing yourself for all our sakes.

(*SCHMINKE grins.*)

SECRETARY-GENERAL: Now he's laughing.

MEDICAL ADVISOR: Who is?

SECRETARY-GENERAL: There. Him.

PRESIDENT: (*Nervously.*) What him? I can't see a him. Can anybody here see a him? Please, ladies and gentlemen, if you see a him, please stand up!

(*Nobody stands up.*)

No one. No one here can see anything. (*To ALFRED.*) Maybe you can see him?

ALFRED: Nooooo.
GIRL: I heard something.
PRESIDENT: What did you hear?
SCHMINKE: Me.
CAPTAIN: (*Standing up.*) Good heavens, I heard something too. (*He suddenly points to SCHMINKE.*) There! Him! You know what, I think he's a Jew.
SECRETARY-GENERAL: He, however, maintains he is an idea.
PRESIDENT: How did the Jew get in?
SECRETARY-GENERAL: He maintains that if the bourgeois stranglehold on society was removed then the resultant prostitution would disappear along with it. Terrible!
PRESIDENT: A Bolshevik.
MEDICAL ADVISOR: How stupid can you get!
CHAIRWOMAN: Prostitution is too deeply anchored in mankind.
ALFRED: Quite right.
CHAIRWOMAN: If you will pardon me for saying so, any change to the bourgeois stranglehold would not have any resultant effect at all on prostitution. To give everything a material reason is to deny the soul.
(*SCHMINKE laughs.*)
DELEGATE: Don't you laugh, young man! I am a secondary school teacher in Lisbon and if you were just twenty years older you would think quite differently.
SCHMINKE: About what?
TEACHER: About God.
SCHMINKE: Hardly.
TEACHER: Just wait and see. (*He starts declaiming.*) Death came quickly to the man…
SCHMINKE: (*Interrupting.*) I'm not a man, I'm an idea. You fool!
TEACHER: (*Yelling.*) Point of order!
ALL: Bravo! Quite right! Too true!
SECRETARY-GENERAL: (*Standing up.*) Point of order. (*He sits down.*)

FOURTH DELEGATE: (*Standing up.*) Let us not allow ourselves to be swayed. The Congress insists on co-operating with the people. I would be truly delighted if that co-operation continued with commercial enterprise…

PRESIDENT: (*Interrupting him.*) The economy!

FOURTH DELEGATE: Of course, the economy.

SCHMINKE: Capital investment.

PRESIDENT: Of course, capital investment. I will not allow these constant self-evident truths.

FOURTH DELEGATE: Who would not delight in reconciling the fine and manual work of capital, with value placed on the protection of culture?! Point of order.

FIRST DELEGATE: If I could bother you for the vegetables…?

MEDICAL ADVISOR: Please!

FIRST DELEGATE: Thank you!

(*Eating, drinking and making merry.*)

SCHMINKE: I would ask the Congress not to forget the girl.

(*The TEACHER throws his fork down on the floor in anger. Eating, drinking and making merry.*)

CHAIRWOMAN: (*Standing up.*) If I could be permitted to move onto the second question, as we are now assured that this person sold herself of her own free will.

SCHMINKE: You are lying!

CHAIRWOMAN: (*Shrieking.*) I will not have this! I will not!

SCHMINKE: You know that the girl is nothing more than a sacrificial lamb on the altar of the bourgeois stranglehold!

CHAIRWOMAN: (*Still squealing.*)

To work for the majority is the duty of man.
Do it without thanks and be glad if you can.
Lazybones and spoilers do not like success.
If they're at your heels, you're certainly not blessed!

(*She collapses on her chair and sobs.*)

PRESIDENT: (*To SCHMINKE.*) What do you want here?

SCHMINKE: To prove that you're a cheat and a fraud!
PRESIDENT: Point of order!
CHAIRWOMAN: Point of order!
SECRETARY-GENERAL: (*Standing up.*) A terrible word has just been uttered. The word 'cheat'. If we accept the argument of an irresponsible professional heckler that economic necessity forced the girl to sell herself, we nevertheless weaken every unpleasantness with the humble understanding, that no man has the power to remove economic necessity, not even the Congress! (*He empties his glass of champagne.*)
ALL: Hear! Hear!
SCHMINKE: Just don't get 'original sin' mixed up with 'capitalism'.
ALFRED: For my part, I believe in the Lord.
SCHMINKE: Well, you should know.
ALFRED: The good Lord helps one and not the other.
SCHMINKE: One should organise the good Lord a little better.
ALFRED: I don't think that's possible.
SCHMINKE: Did He help you?
ALFRED: Thanks be to God.
SCHMINKE: (*Grinning.*) I'm beginning to like that good Lord more and more…
PRESIDENT: Point of order!
SECRETARY-GENERAL: (*Swallowing another glass of champagne in one.*) I'm already hoarse, but giddy up. Not only this girl, but millions of girls like her could be said to suffer from absolutely the same typical poverty – yet not all resort to selling themselves. We are now approaching the psychological core of the matter. So let's ask the girl: why do you sell yourself? Why don't you kill yourself?
OLD-FASHIONED DELEGATE: If I was forced to choose between prostitution and death…
CHAIRWOMAN: (*Leaping to her feet and interrupting shrilly.*) Gentlemen! We would all prefer to kill ourselves!
ALL: Bravo! Bravo!
GIRL: I did want to commit suicide once, but then I thought, it's better to sell myself. It's easier.

(*Pause.*)

OLD-FASHIONED DELEGATE: Can she be described as human?

TEACHER: Is this shameless hussy devoid of any shame?

PRESIDENT: Please, I beg you, remember there are ladies present.

TEACHER: I am shaking with…

OLD-FASHIONED DELEGATE: (*To the SECRETARY-GENERAL.*) Would you be so kind to ask that person if she understand the expression 'pure love'.

SECRETARY-GENERAL: Fraülein, do you understand the…

GIRL: (*Interrupting him.*) No.

SECRETARY-GENERAL: And why not?

GIRL: Because it does not exist.

(*The CAPTAIN laughs loudly.*)

OLD-FASHIONED DELEGATE: Charming!

SECRETARY-GENERAL: Take very good care, Fraülein! And how do you know that there is no such thing as pure love?

GIRL: I was married once.

TEACHER: Is that true?

GIRL: In a church. But not for long.

SECRETARY-GENERAL: But why not for long?

PRESIDENT: Please reveal all – but not for too long.

GIRL: My husband was an extremely moral man. He had a tobacconist shop and divorced me because I went to a garden party with a stranger. My husband's name was Ferdinand.

PRESIDENT: Go on!

GIRL: Then the stranger left me too, because after a while I got on his nerves. I think he was a cad.

CAPTAIN: That is how you become a cad, ladies and gentlemen!

TEACHER: Quite right! In truth!

CAPTAIN: A cabaret!

PRESIDENT: (*Cynically.*) And now, Fraülein, you are looking to get married again in a church?

(*The MEDICAL ADVISOR giggles.*)

GIRL: No.
SECRETARY-GENERAL: Why not?
GIRL: I just didn't know he was going to leave me straight after. Now I'm no longer angry with him.
PRESIDENT: (*Mockingly.*) You don't say!
GIRL: His name was Arthur.
OLD-FASHIONED DELEGATE: Carry on!
GIRL: And that's how things went for a while.
PRESIDENT: How did they go?
GIRL: I didn't have a thing.
PRESIDENT: (*Grinning.*) No Arthur?
GIRL: No money.
MEDICAL ADVISOR: Anyone who wants to work, can.
SCHMINKE: Excuse me, are you not the medical advisor?
MEDICAL ADVISOR: Yes. So what?
SCHMINKE: Your father owned a factory?
MEDICAL ADVISOR: Anyone who wants to work, can.
SCHMINKE: And you're married to the daughter of a jeweller from the Bremserstrasse.
MEDICAL ADVISOR: (*Yelling at SCHMINKE.*) Anyone who wants to work, can!
GIRL: I couldn't.
MEDICAL ADVISOR: (*Slamming his fist down on the table.*) I won't have this!
(*The GIRL shrugs her shoulders.*)
PRESIDENT: All this not being able is not very compelling.
(*The GIRL shrugs her shoulders.*)
TEACHER: A lazy Lolita.
MEDICAL ADVISOR: Degenerate.
OLD-FASHIONED DELEGATE: (*To the SECRETARY-GENERAL.*) Sir, would you be so kind to ask this degenerate person if she takes any pleasure from the practice of her sinful trade?
GIRL: You're joking.
ALFRED: (*Looking at his watch.*) May I point out to the Congress that the Fraülein needs to embark soon. Time is pressing. If I could ask for the questions to be…

PRESIDENT: (*Interrupting him.*) I believe the Congress has no desire for further questions. We are appalled at this case of extraordinary hard-heartedness.

SCHMINKE: So when will you be made Social Security Secretary?

PRESIDENT: Point of order!

SECRETARY-GENERAL: Alfred, sir. I am particularly pleased and honoured to be able to thank you deeply on behalf of the International Congress for the International Fight against International Prostitution for putting yourself out in order to help us. Your solid professional experience has given the Congress new weapons, new courage, new stamina to wage a Homeric war against the Hydra of prostitution. It will be a bloody battle, after all, we are seeking an absolute victory of the irrational over the rational!

SCHMINKE: Bravo!

SECRETARY-GENERAL: I raise my glass and wish you well.

(*He drinks to ALFRED.*

ALFRED bows to the Congress.

The Congress applauds.

Music.

The Congress rises, because there's nothing left to eat or drink and the banquet has come to an end.

The band plays a lively military march.

The SECRETARY-GENERAL walks over to ALFRED and shakes his hand.)

I would be extremely grateful if you would fill out this form regarding the technicalities of the white slave trade. (*He hands him a form.*) The form is printed, because we want around five thousand people involved in prostitution to fill it in.

ALFRED: As a point of order.

SECRETARY-GENERAL: And I just wanted to...(*He hands him an envelope.*) Here is your fee.

ALFRED: (*Counting the money and putting it away, satisfied.*) It is an honour and pleasure to thank you on behalf of myself.

(*The SECRETARY-GENERAL bows.*
ALFRED slaps him on the back.)
Should you need me again, I would be delighted to offer the Congress my wisdom and experience. It's quite likely that I am to sell a widowed brunette to Santa Fe de Bogota in two weeks' time and...

SECRETARY-GENERAL: I'll be in touch.
(*He shakes his hand, bows, spots SCHMINKE and glares at him.*)

AN ELEGANT DELEGATE: Herr Alfred! I would be more than delighted if you could join me on Thursday evening. May I expect you? I am organising a small private concert in aid of endangered young women. My uncle received first prize in the 'Most Beautiful Car' competition.
(*ALFRED kisses her hand.*)

CAPTAIN: (*Welsh. To the ELEGANT DELEGATE.*) Excuse me, your ladyship, may I proffer you my arm – I've just found the cold buffet. (*He exits with her.*)

ALFRED: Now there's a jealous soldier. (*He fills in the questionnaire.*)

SECRETARY-GENERAL: (*To SCHMINKE.*) May I enquire, are you finally going to leave or not?

SCHMINKE: Don't make a fool of yourself.

SECRETARY-GENERAL: You have embarrassed me thoroughly throughout the banquet. The food turned to dust in my mouth. And now it's time for the cold buffet. Do you want to continue to ruin my appetite?

SCHMINKE: I'm not that mean.

SECRETARY-GENERAL: You appear even more so. Please, let me relax, we've come to the social part.

SCHMINKE: (*Smirking.*) I enjoy socialising.
(*Pause.*)

SECRETARY-GENERAL: (*Smirking.*) People will have to get used to you. Just do not harbour the hope that an inner conflict will destroy me. I can tell you that in my role as Secretary-General. Oh yes! (*He leaves him standing there.*)
(*The Congress slowly heads towards the buffet.*)

GIRL: (*To ALFRED, who is still filling in the questionnaire.*) When can I leave?

ALFRED: Straightaway.

GIRL: Time is pressing.

ALFRED: I know.

GIRL: Just don't bring me to something like this ever again. I'd rather go with a man with a false leg than come here.

ALFRED: Shush, girl. This is a pretty complicated questionnaire.

GIRL: This whole questioning business is pointless – they don't believe what you say, they just get all excited.

ALFRED: Nonsense. You're being paid for it. Here, you can have your two marks.

GIRL: But you said three...

ALFRED: To err is human!

(*Pause.*)

GIRL: I'm hungry.

ALFRED: Please control yourself! Alright?

GIRL: (*Suddenly spotting something.*) He's coming.

ALFRED: Who?

GIRL: Our Ferdinand.

(*FERDINAND appears and bows to the GIRL. The GIRL nods.*)

FERDINAND: (*Quietly.*) Alfred.

ALFRED: (*Also quietly.*) What?

(*The GIRL listens.*)

FERDINAND: I've been thinking.

ALFRED: About what?

FERDINAND: The South American deal.

ALFRED: And what's that supposed to mean?

FERDINAND: It means, I'm asking you to return the half of my good Lord.

ALFRED: Are you mad?

FERDINAND: No, but from the purely human point of view. I wasn't to know that we were selling this girl...

ALFRED: From the purely human point of view we shouldn't be selling girls at all!

FERDINAND: That's different. You see, I'm so human that anything humanity does, I understand. And that's why I understand how one can sell a girl – I don't damn it but in certain circumstances, also take part. But this girl in particular – she and I were once very close.

ALFRED: Shush! Business is business!

FERDINAND: I'll sell everyone, just not that one. I don't know why. It's not sentimentality. God alone knows what it could be!

ALFRED: Shush! If I were to give you back the half of your good Lord – well, what are you going to do about the cafetière?

(*FERDINAND stares at him.*)

Your cafetière of coffee?

(*FERDINAND is speechless.*)

You did say you were doing it all for a cafetière...

FERDINAND: Of course, the cafetière...

ALFRED: Wake up! Smell the coffee! Cup or cafetière?

(*Pause.*)

FERDINAND: (*After an internal struggle.*) Cup.

ALFRED: Never again will you have a cafetière...

FERDINAND: (*Interrupting him angrily.*) Fine! Then no more cafetières for me!

SCHMINKE: Stop! You can drink your cafetière. You seem to have forgotten that the individual person cannot be helped, as a matter of principle!

GIRL: Is that what you think?

SCHMINKE: Yes!

FERDINAND: (*Recognising SCHMINKE.*) As a matter of principle...

SCHMINKE: According to the inexorable laws of capitalism, the girl has to end up in South America. Ill, demoralised and brutalised!

ALFRED: Did you hear that?

FERDINAND: As a matter of principle...

SCHMINKE: We are looking at a typical case of...

FERDINAND: (*Interrupting him.*) Well, let's look at it then! I hereby declare in the strongest possible terms that

I relinquish the half of my good Lord, that the girl and I remarry, and that with the other half of my good Lord I will start a small tobacco shop and that never again will I aspire to a cafetière of coffee!

SCHMINKE: (*To the SECRETARY-GENERAL.*) Sir, did you hear that!

SECRETARY-GENERAL: Did I hear what?

SCHMINKE: The girl is not to be sold but to be married.

SECRETARY-GENERAL: Oho! Point of order!

FERDINAND: Excuse me. I'm a stranger to these parts and don't know my way around. Who is that?

SECRETARY-GENERAL: The Congress.

FERDINAND: For the fight against the white slave trade?

SECRETARY-GENERAL: Oh yes!

FERDINAND: So it will be delighted to hear that I have succeeded in rescuing the girl.

SECRETARY-GENERAL: Point of order!

SCHMINKE: I protest. The so-called humanity of this man is falsifying the actual state of affairs.

SECRETARY-GENERAL: In the name of the Congress, I add my voice to this protest. Where would we be if we paid forty-eight marks to study a prostitute and then discover that we have only shone a light into the life of a petit-bourgeois married woman! I would have been a Secretary-General years ago if that was the case! You with your humanity have no right to cut a swathe through the ordered process of the fight against the white slave trade! Oh yes!

ALFRED: I couldn't agree with you more, Secretary-General sir! I have already signed the contract with the company Ibanez in Parana. Apart from the fine, my reputation as a businessman would be brought into disrepute. Idiot.

FERDINAND: (*To the GIRL.*) Am I an idiot?

GIRL: No.

FERDINAND: What?

GIRL: No.

SCHMINKE: Quite right!

SECRETARY-GENERAL: God be praised.

ALFRED: Bravo!
FERDINAND: No...?
GIRL: When I saw you in Café Rump, I shrieked, because I was so shocked – about the past, because it was suddenly here. You see, I thought that everything inside me was broken, but since then everything is whole again. I can't explain it any better. The gentlemen here are quite right. I can't go back, because: because it would all be so different and I don't want it to be different. I've reached a point of no return.
ALFRED: (*Glancing at the clock.*) Time is pressing...
FERDINAND: (*To the GIRL.*) Most peculiar. Don't you have anything else to say to me?
GIRL: Just drink your cafetière.
FERDINAND: I think not. It doesn't appeal any more.
ALFRED: Then let's go! Or we'll be late!
A MEMBER OF THE AUDIENCE: Stop! I protest against this deception!
ALFRED: Don't meddle in other people's affairs, sir! Who are you, anyway?
A MEMBER OF THE AUDIENCE: I'm sitting over there in the second row! I bought a ticket because the theatre hoarding said 'farce in five scenes'. And suddenly I'm watching a tragic ending! I won't have it! That is misrepresentation!
SCHMINKE: That is truth. The terrible truth!
A MEMBER OF THE AUDIENCE: Then I can manage without the truth! I'm a tired working man and want to watch a farce of an evening! Understand? Either I have my farce or you can give me my money back!
SCHMINKE: With pleasure!
SECRETARY-GENERAL: (*To SCHMINKE.*) Oh shut up!
A MEMBER OF THE AUDIENCE: I want my farce! I suggest: the girl doesn't go to South America but marries Ferdinand instead, and both live happily, healthily and contentedly above their tobacconist!
SCHMINKE: That is pure deception!
A MEMBER OF THE AUDIENCE: Deception is proclaiming a farce and ending up with some tragic pantomime!

ALFRED: (*To SCHMINKE.*) Be gone! Be gone! Be gone!
(*SCHMINKE sits down, pulls a newspaper out of his pocket and reads it.*)

FERDINAND: (*To the MEMBER OF THE AUDIENCE.*) Beg your pardon! You're a good man!

SCHMINKE: (*Reading.*) Escheloher Hanf seven twelve – disappointing result: only a ten per cent dividend.

A MEMBER OF THE AUDIENCE: Well, what are we waiting for?
(*Wedding March.*
FERDINAND is radiant, gathers the GIRL into his arms and kisses her.)
That's right!

CAPTAIN: (*Appearing, he taps FERDINAND on the shoulder.*) Excuse me, dear Ferdinand!

FERDINAND: (*Not letting the GIRL go.*) What is it?

CAPTAIN: There is a lady outside who would like to speak to the happy couple.

GIRL: Please call her in, Captain!
(*The CAPTAIN makes a sign.*)

LUISE: (*Entering in a white dress, she hands the happy couple a huge bouquet.*) My warmest congratulations. (*She burps.*)
(*Everyone starts at the burp.*)

The End.